THE ART OF
BEING AN EXECUTIVE

Louis B. Lundborg

THE FREE PRESS
A Division of Macmillan Publishing Co., Inc.
NEW YORK

Collier Macmillan Publishers
LONDON

The Free Press
A Division of Macmillan Publishing Co., Inc.
866 Third Avenue, New York, N.Y. 10022

Collier Macmillan Canada, Ltd.

Library of Congress Catalog Card Number: 81–66986

Printed in the United States of America

printing number

1 2 3 4 5 6 7 8 9 10

Library of Congress Cataloging in Publication Data

Lundborg, Louis B.
  The art of being an executive.

  Includes index.
  1. Executive ability. I. Title.
HF5500.2.L88   658.4'09   81-66986
ISBN 0-02-919300-1   AACR2

Contents

Preface

This book is not about how a company should be operated. It is about how a chief executive, and the other executives down the line, should operate in managing the company. While the two things overlap, it is primarily about the executive, rather than the company.

Yet the company does not come off second best in this approach. Executives get the best results for their companies by doing the best possible job of being executives. At the same time, they are more likely to preserve their own health and peace of mind as well as advance their companies' well-being if they do a good job of being effective executives than if they do a poor one.

The title of the book was chosen to emphasize that being an executive is an art—not a science.

Early in this century Frederick Taylor coined the phrase "scientific management." What it described was only the smallest fraction of the total function of management—it was concerned only with reducing the time and effort expended in repetitive manual labor. In a day when machines had barely begun to substitute for the drudgery of human labor, Taylor's work had great impact on how industrial operations were conducted and supervised.

The job of managing an enterprise even in that early day, though, embraced much more than just getting physical work done. And as businesses have grown in size and complexity, so has the job of managing them. But in spite of all the technology that has been brought to the aid of management, management itself has not become a science. Computer-based management information systems may deliver exquisitely refined streams of information on every aspect of the company, its industry, its markets, and the world economy. But the decisions made on the basis of that information are still made by human beings, not by the machines. More than that, the information itself is never complete: management still remains the art of making decisions on the basis of less than complete information. The executive at any level—whether in sales, in marketing, in finance, or in top management—who waits until he has the last morsel of information will never make a decision. The competitive world will pass him by while he sits waiting.

That is why it is the art, not the science, of management. Human decision makers apply their best judgment to a complex of variables that are never the same twice. Each decision is a unique assembling of pieces that one fits together as an artist creates a painting or a mosaic. So the parallel to the language of art is not inappropriate. And as with the visual artist, the resulting creation may be a success, and it may not. In both cases, the market applies the test.

Within that process sits the individual executive. His role is much more personal than this talk of management information systems and decision-making processes would suggest. The executive does make decisions, of course; but a large part of what he does is to lead and encourage and orchestrate the work of others who make it possible for the big decisions to have any meaning.

This book is about those personal things—those bits and pieces of the picture that make up the art of being an executive.

In planning and writing this book, no consideration was given to separate treatment of the managerial problems of women. The assumption at the outset, followed throughout the book, was that of the many ingredients in the art of being an executive, none was sex-differentiated. All of them would be made easier or harder to acquire by differences in temperamental and emotional habits and characteristics; but the range of those differences is as great within each sex as it is between the two sexes.

So the approach has been "work with what you've got"—whatever that was.

This approach led to another early-on decision of convenience (convenience to the reader as well as to the writer): to treat such words as "man" and "he" as generic terms.

The assumption, again, was that it is as wearying to the reader as it is to the writer to have a succession of "he or she," "him or her," "man or woman" clichés. They interrupt thought more than they clarify it. So until the English language finds some new, vital bridge-words for this context, I must simply ask forgiveness for any offense that my generic use of masculine terms may cause.

A Boss for All Seasons

Think of him as "Louie," the way his friends have always done. That's not because he was ever the buddy-buddy type or the office glad-hander. No, he was quite the opposite, reserved and precise. He'd turn downright chilly if anyone seemed a little sloppy in thought or behavior. He hated sham of any sort, or the faintest whiff of dishonesty. And his teeth would grate at a hint of bigotry, or the standard macho haw-haws that used to pass for executive-suite humor. As the chairman of the world's biggest bank, California's Bank of America, his aversions carried considerable weight. In fact, when he became the first top-rank American business executive to testify in Congress against the Vietnam War, quite a few other executives got pretty hot at his influence.

Looking back now, Louis B. Lundborg seems to have been the least likely person in the world to become a sort of managerial cult figure. But such a process had already begun at the time of his death from lung cancer early this year. The "Lundborg ethic" will live for years among young executives who never even met him. I should have seen it coming. Within a few days after his death, a young Iranian refugee who has studied Louie's career from a distance called me to say, with considerable anger, that none of us older people seemed to have understood how unique he was.

I'd first run across Lundborg followers among Japan's best and brightest. Louie was, in fact, more widely known there than in his home country. His famous book of top-management dialogues with Kohnosuke Matsushita, Japan's living legend of executive wisdom, became a best-seller in Tokyo, Osaka, and other industrial centers. Louie's picture began to pop up in both professional and popular journals.

People could somehow sense, even across the language barrier, that here was a man of deep and passionate understanding. As Peter Drucker once remarked, he carried on the populist tradition of banking as well as the man-to-man tradition in management. When I helped Avis President Robert Townsend on the savage humor of his *Up the Organization* book, Louie loved the laughter but did not care for the book's anger. It took the humanity out of it, he felt, and to him that was not to be tolerated.

Louie found his natural style in "Executive Survival Kit," his regular column for *Industry Week* magazine. Not at all sure he wanted to do it, he first tested a few short essays before he began to sense how much he had to say that nobody else was saying. And soon he hit stride. The more mundane the question he wrestled with, the more he delighted in passing along the seasoned wisdom of his sixty years of work. This book is largely based on the ideas he first developed as columns, but when time came to do the manuscript he started all over. Always a quality addict, he now knew things he'd not quite seen when he did the columns, and there were new subjects he just had to cover. He worked with total focus until he finished the manuscript just before lung cancer—which he had gallantly kept hidden even from his secretary—suddenly cut his life down to four days.

This book reflects the breadth and depth of his experience and the quality of his thought. Having lent money to every kind of business, he knew better than most how small flaws can grow into big troubles. Yet, he never lost that quick gift of irony and laughter. This shy gentlemen, 6'1" in his neat pinstripes, shares useful knowhow with us on every page.

Before becoming chairman, Mr. Lundborg was part of the management team that led the Bank of America out of California isolation into its new era in competition with Eastern and Midwestern commercial banks. He played a strategic role in launching BankAmericard—now VISA, the most universal bank payment system in the world.

As a friend, I watched Louis over the years with rising awe at his insights and accomplishments. "All that got done," he says, "was done through other people,"

That remark comes less from his modesty than out of his ruthless honesty about the job of the effective manager. A manager must be a teacher, or, as Louis carefully insists, one who helps others to grow.

Son of threadbare Swedish immigrants, Mr. Lundborg grew up on a potato homestead in a Montana log cabin. After working his way through Stanford, Louis got a look at California's booming industry as a Chamber of Commerce officer before heading back to Stanford as a vice president and then settling down to learn the business of banking.

Characteristically, Louis considered one of the most significant events of his business career his encounters with student radicals after a mob burned a bank branch in Santa Barbara and other students attacked branches throughout the state. Chairman Lundborg threw himself into the center of the storm by meeting and listening to protest leaders all over California.

The result profoundly changed and renewed him. Perhaps the last word on Louis's contribution to management comes from his close friend Walter A. Haas, Jr., Chairman of Levi-Strauss & Company, who teamed with Louis in many efforts to develop the concept of corporate social responsibility:

> Louis Lundborg was, to me, the epitome of a socially responsible business executive. He recognized the need for change in

business' role in our total society and spoke up about that need in his roles as a writer, teacher, television series host and, most importantly, Chairman of the Board of the world's largest bank. I had the good fortune to serve on the board Lou chaired and to head that board's Social Responsibility Committee and will always treasure the memory of our great relationship. He assumed a leadership role in reacting to the expectations of the public and the increasing social and political pressures placed on the business community. The way he did this established him as an individual of integrity with vision and, most importantly, a genuine concern for people.

T George Harris

First Things First— Managing Yourself

Being an executive has many parts. Some of them are independent of each other: you do them or you don't; and if you don't do them, you won't get as good marks as you could on your executive-performance report card.

But some others are part of the life process—like breathing and keeping the heart beating. If you don't do them, you don't survive long as an executive; but if you *do* do them, you make everything else work much more smoothly.

The first section of the book deals with those "central life process" ingredients.

Manage Thyself

Q You have talked about a lot of things that are important parts of the executive's job; and of course they all are important. But can you say what is *the* most important part of the job? If an executive had to pick and choose among competing demands on his time, what is the one thing he could not eliminate?

A Easy. At least, easy to spell out; not so easy for you to do. But much easier than trying to do your job without doing this first.

The first thing an executive has to manage is himself. If he doesn't manage his own time, his own priorities, he won't have a chance to manage the company as he should. So I put that first in *my* priorities.

If he has harnessed that one, the order of the next ones won't matter, because he will know that he has to reserve the right amounts of time, energy, and attention to each of the others. Of course, if he does this part of his job right, the "right" amount of time to spend on some things will be zero.

How do you go about setting up priorities? The details vary; but everyone I know who has been successful in managing his time and himself has done something like this: The first thing he does, before he can make good decisions on how to use his time, is to ask and answer a more basic question, "What do I really want most out of my life? What do I want to accomplish, and what do I want to have as a life style?"

You can call these your goals or your objectives or your whatever, but they are the standards against which you measure all your choices. Part of your answer will involve your business:

> Do you want to be president of your company?
>
> If you already are, do you want to make it the biggest in its field? Or do you only want a bigger share of the market? Or are you content to hold your present market share?
>
> Do you want to have a business of your own?
>
> Do you have some other major business target?

Do you have specific goals for your family and the time you will spend with them:

> Where do you want to live?
>
> How do you want to vacation?
>
> What hobbies do you want to pursue?
>
> How much time, and *which* time, do you want to spend with your children? With your wife?

There is nothing wrong with including family values in your goals as an executive. In fact, if you don't—and if you are not honest with yourself about the relative weight that you give to each of these goals—you will be in constant conflict. There are tradeoffs, and prices to be paid for each tradeoff, on every such choice. But the price is far less if the choices are made against a set of values than if each one is made on its own with no guidelines.

These are your priorities. You can achieve as much of each one of them as you want, if you manage yourself and are willing to pay the price for each of the choices. So choose your priorities carefully: if you live by them, they will rule your life. But that is better, far better, than having your life ruled by the pressures, the whims, and the priorities of others that you let them impose on you.

While there is no single pattern of priorities that will guarantee success (and I would not presume to prescribe a standard-package formula for everyone), it is my observation that in today's complex world business executives succeed better if their priorities are not all weighted toward business goals. Paradoxically, the greater the pressure of the business demands, the more essential it is to get away from those demands on a regular basis—to get complete detachment for self-renewal. You may get it with family, with friends, with whatever interests recharge your batteries and restore perspective. But the more you strive to maintain that balance between stress and release, the more essential it is to have priorities.

Once you know what your priorities are, it is easy to sort out the demands on your time and energy. You will find them falling into three categories:

> *Top priority:* central concerns and essential activities that will contribute to the achieving of your goals are central. Along with these are a few life-support and maintenance activities you can't dodge without penalty: brushing your teeth, shaving (if you're a man), catching your plane, etc.

Medium priority: secondary matters—those that are fine, worthwhile things in themselves but contribute nothing right now toward what you most want to accomplish.

Bottom priority: marginal matters. Some of these are distractions that others have pushed at you—invitations, requests, letters, etc., that have no attraction or importance to you, except that you are afraid you'll offend someone if you ignore or decline them. But some are of your own making, like the desk top, workroom, or garage that needs straightening or the hobby collection that needs organizing.

The key to managing this part of your life is your attitude: decide to do what you think is the right mix of activities—but not because someone else has pushed you or because you will feel guilty if you don't. There is nothing wrong with allocating some of your time to marginal, low-priority, or secondary affairs, if you decide that that is how you would most like to spend that part of your time that you are saving for yourself. In that case, don't feel guilty about it—enjoy it. But above all, don't feel guilty about the marginal and secondary things you *don't* do. If you never do them, that is soon enough.

If you are a typical executive, the demands on your time will total several times what you can do. I used to say that I could have been four people: I could have spent 100% of my time at my desk, 100% out among our branch and department officers and employees, 100% calling on customers, and 100% in civic and public affairs and contacts. For a while I tried being all four, jumping without plan from one to another, getting none of them done well and driving myself frantic in the process. It was only after I devised my own test, to see which of these competing demands deserved top priority, that I restored some sanity to the process.

Each of us should apply the test that works best for him. Dru Scott, the psychologist who writes, lectures and counsels on time management, has devised one method that she calls the "One Hundredth Birthday Technique": imagine that you are being interviewed by a newspaper reporter on your 100th birthday and asked to name your most important accomplishments. How would you like to be able to answer? And which of the things you are currently trying to decide about would contribute to that accomplishment that you would like to claim?

For myself, I settled on a shorter-range test: "Which way will the bank be better off five years from now—if I do this or if I don't?" Where it involved conflict with family concerns, I would ask myself, "Which way will my family be better off five years from now—if I do this or if I don't?" It was amazing how quickly it sorted things out: what had seemed terribly urgent on a right-now basis might evaporate into nothing in the perspective of five years. Or what seemed like a painful sacrifice right now might seem very much worth doing, for the five-year return.

Time Wasters

Q How do I keep other people from wasting my time? I have outsiders coming to see me from community organizations, as well as people from my own company. I feel I have to see most of these people, and I really want to. But some of them stay so long that they take too big a chunk out of my day.

A The hardest part is not to defeat your purpose in seeing them: if you make them feel too unwelcome, you might as well tell them "I'm too busy to see you" and be done with it.

You would be treating them the way Ray Lyman Wilbur treated students who came to see him when he was president of Stanford University. He would look up from the papers on his desk long enough to listen to what the student had to say. He would give his answer. Then, if he decided that was the end of the conversation, he would simply go back to the papers on his desk. No "good day," "thank you," or "excuse me." The student just didn't exist any more. Efficient, yes. But it neither made friends for Wilbur nor gave the student any feeling of self-confidence.

I never like "techniques" in dealing with people. They smack of artificiality, and that you don't want. But there are honest, straightforward steps you can take. Here are some of the things that are done by people who have mastered this problem:

First, when your friend calls for an appointment, ask, "How long will we need? My day is chopped up in pieces" (that will always be true, hence honest) "but I really want to see you— let's see when we can do it."

Then, when he gets there, seem genuinely glad to see him and interested in his problem—not pained or bored. But don't initiate gossipy conversation that will start him off on a long-winded tangent. The minute he sits down, ask him, "What have we got today?" If you want to ask him about his wife and kids, do it after you are both standing and moving toward the door.

Keep your own responses crisp and help to keep him on the track. Don't let either of you wander off course. If you arrive at a good answer, "close." Ask him, "Does that do it?" and tell him again how glad you were to see him.

If you can see that you are not getting anywhere, try to give him an alternative course of action. "I think you should next try so and so. . . ." If there *isn't* any alternative you can see, if you are just spinning your wheels, find some early way of saying so: "I just don't think I have an answer to that."

If he is asking you to do something you know you are not going to do, don't let him waste too much of his own time—let alone yours. Tell him, "I know I can't do it, so I'd better let you get quickly on to your next choice." If you have alternate suggestions, fine—give them to him, and suggest that he follow up promptly on them.

I have two friends who know that they can see me any time they want to, and on very short notice. One will call me and say, "I need just eight minutes"—and at the end of seven and a half minutes he is on his feet and started out the door with his business done. It may be twelve or sixteen minutes—but I always know it will never be a minute more than he asked for.

The other will appear with a typed agenda that he will lay before me: "These are the things I want to discuss with you. If there are any you don't want to talk about or haven't time for today, cross them off." We then go through them bing-bing-bing and he is on his way.

Inside your own organization you can find a dozen ways to get the message over that you like to have things thought out and organized ahead of time in some such way as that. Failing all else, just say it plain and clear in a staff meeting. But usually the grapevine will pick it up if you really mean it.

With the outsiders, you will have to find slightly different ways to communicate—but only slightly. The community grapevine isn't so different from the company grapevine. You can plant the message and it will spread. One of the best ways, of course, is to compliment the ones who do things the way you like them: they'll spread the word.

Ration yourself on the number of visitors you see in a day or a week. Don't be shy about making them wait. The ones you really want to eliminate should be politely told at the outset that you are not going to be able to see them in the foreseeable future. The others then should be spaced out at a rate that you can digest—and at a rate that fits in with your scale of priorities.

The Life of Your Time

Q You have made helpful suggestions on how to deal with outside time wasters. But even when I think I have handled that part of my time problem, I still don't seem to have good control of my time. At the end of a day or a week I just haven't had time to get the things done that I had hoped to do. How can I lick that?

A Remember that you have the same amount of time as everyone else. No one can have any more, and you need not have any less. And it all belongs to you, to use as you choose. The trouble is that most of us do not choose: we either let someone else do the choosing—we let someone else eat up our time—or we ourselves let it slip through our fingers without even knowing it is going, or where.

Right there is the hub of most people's time problem: they do not know where it is going, or even where it went after it is gone. You may not like the prospect of having to be a minute-pincher, counting out your minutes and hours like a miser counting out his pieces of silver and gold. But if you do it, you

11

will be joining a distinguished company: I know of no effective executive who has not made a conscious point of managing his time as deliberately as an investor manages his securities.

Most of them start by keeping track—logging what they do every minute of the day for two or three weeks. Some of them get so in the habit that they go right on doing it. Professionals, such as attorneys and accountants who do their billing entirely on the basis of time spent on each client account, typically keep a time sheet, diary, or log book on their desks at all times. Some have their secretaries keep the record. They can tell at the end of a day—or at the end of a year—just how their time has been spent: how much that is billable to each client, how much on nonbillable activities. Many nonprofessionals use the same kind of sheets. Whatever the recording method, two rules should be absolute: the recording should be done at the moment ("in real time"), not at the end of the day or the next day, when memory will play deceptive tricks; and, unless you are going to make the log a continuous practice, it should be repeated every few months—at least twice a year. New pressures and old habits can combine to make you drift back into wasteful patterns.

I have used a variant that has been helpful to me and might be to others. Instead of just recording how my time has been spent, I have started at the beginning of the day by estimating how much time I was going to spend on each activity of the day. I would know what meetings and appointments I had, and I would estimate how much time each of those *should* take—how much they were "entitled to." Then I knew what else I wanted to get done during the day, and how long I needed for each part. Even at that point I was assigning priorities and trying to match time allocation to priority. Then I kept track of how long I actually spent on each of these undertakings—plus the unexpected and unallocated interruptions: mostly phone calls plus whatever followup I thought I had to make on each call; and an occasional visitor whom I felt obliged to see.

At first I was appalled by the discrepancy between what I had projected and what actually happened. It would have been easy to dismiss the whole exercise as nonsense: no one can plan his day so precisely and expect to hold to the plan.

But the value of what I learned had little to do with planning, in the sense of a rigid schedule of time allocations. Even the fact that I had not been accurate or realistic in my estimates of time required was not the most important. What mattered was that I found that I was allowing my time to be frittered away by things of minor importance, while I was not saving—and guarding—the time I should have been spending on the really vital matters.

The next—and the most crucial—question to ask is, "What *are* the really vital matters?" As you review the way you have spent your time—and, in the future, *before* you spend it—ask yourself, "Does it really matter whether I do this or not? Does it matter whether *anybody* does it? Would I, or the company, be missed if nobody attended that luncheon, or dinner, where I spent three hours? If it is important, would it be good experience and good exposure for one of the younger officers?"

That, incidentally, points to the one exception to the rule that time is inelastic and cannot be increased or stretched: you can acquire time by deciding that some of the things you are doing can be done as well or better by others.

A CPM for the CEO

Q You have spoken of the importance of having a CPM (critical path method) or MRP (materials requirement plan) in a manufacturing company, so that all the component parts and "bits and pieces" of a product or project will come together at the right time. There is no question that that can avoid the costly delays that come when some critical ingredient doesn't arrive in time and everything grinds to a halt.

But isn't some equivalent just as essential in a nonmanufacturing company?

A It is—and not only in the nonmanufacturing company but also in the nonmanufacturing activities of the industrial concern. Let's start with that one first, with the most critical of all activities: those of the CEO himself.

One of the first essentials for a chief executive is that he be a planner. Yet some executives who do a good job of future planning for their companies do not do an equally good job of scheduling the things they have to do personally, or the things that will require their approval before others can proceed. The result can be extra stress on the executive himself from the frenzy of last-minute deadline pushing; or extra stress on others from the frustration of not being able to meet schedules—plus the risk of actual company loss from failure to meet commitments.

So the CEO needs to have his own "CPM" to remind him how much lead time he will need for each element of his major commitments and responsibilities. For example, at the annual shareholders' meeting he must be prepared to answer questions from the floor on every aspect of his business. If he wants to be sure that he is current and accurate in all his answers, he will want to have one or more briefing sessions with the people on whom he depends to keep him informed and advised; and he may also want a ready-reference book prepared, with this same and other factual material, that he can keep at his elbow during the meeting.

If all this is to come together smoothly, a group of his advisers must begin conferring weeks before the meeting—first to identify all the types of questions that might be likely to be asked in the annual meeting. Some of these will be entirely factual, some will deal with company policies and attitudes, and some will get into the realm of political or other public-policy questions in which the company may be involved. So the next step is to identify who should take responsibility for developing each of the necessary pieces of actual data and policy papers.

Since each of these will have a different timetable, and since the CEO will need to calculate how much time he will need to digest each of these pieces—and will need to fit that time into the rest of his schedule—he will have to come into these preliminary planning discussions early enough that realistic deadlines can be set.

While he should lean on his staff to do the spade work of putting the pieces together, his early sessions with his planning group permit him not only to set timetables but to indicate the areas where he wants greater emphasis or depth.

The same scenario, with a different cast of characters in each case, needs to be played out in one setting after another through the corporate year: adoption of the business plan for the year, corporate and strategic plans for longer periods, budgets for each period, compensation programs, executive evaluation and projection reviews, preparation of the annual report—these are all typical. And since these overlap all through the year, it becomes doubly important that they be "traffic-managed." Otherwise the people involved will be falling all over themselves and each other in confusion; and the CEO himself will be caught in the backwash of their confusion.

So the CEO's critical path method should be a master calendar for the year that plots out the starting times, lead times, and target dates for everything in which he has a primary role.

Such a master calendar has the added value that when he is asked to do something new and unscheduled, he can tell at a glance whether it will conflict with something important. If it does, he can either decline or know that he must step up his advance planning. At least he will not be caught later in a last-minute crisis.

In a company of any size and complexity, there are as many decision streams flowing out of or near the CEO's office as there are production streams flowing into the factory's assembly lines. I hope the CEO in your company is not making too many of those decisions himself; but if he has not made the right provisions for those decisions to be made by someone else—and at the right time—they can become bottlenecks that will upset rhythms all over the company. They might even have an impact on the production-line timetables; but at the very least they will put unnecessary pressures, frustrations, and stresses on the people who are waiting for the decisions.

P.S. Here is something to add to the procedure for getting the CEO briefed for his annual shareholders' meeting: Many accounting firms have prepared booklets summarizing the questions likely to be asked at shareholders' meetings. These have been based in part on questions asked in previous years and in part on an appraisal of current issues most likely to produce questions in the current year.

While not all these questions are pertinent to any one company, I suggest that those preparing for the annual meeting run through one of these booklets as a checklist.

The Paper Chase

Q I have a fairly orderly mind in other respects, but one thing has me stumped: my handling of my paperwork. And because my secretary has some of the same bad habits I have, we are always hunting for papers that have gotten buried or mislaid somewhere. It not only wastes a lot of time, but it has gotten me into trouble with people who were waiting for answers or action. Do you have any advice on how to lick this problem?

A Start with a couple of pieces of answers that may get you pointed in the right direction.

The most valuable lesson I have learned in how to avoid the frustration and the time that is wasted hunting for things that get buried under "clutter" was taught me by my brother, the engineer and home craftsman. Carl makes beautiful furniture and exquisite carvings of birds and animals; and in the process he uses dozens of tools for cutting, measuring, clamping, gluing, polishing, and the like. But there is never a tool on his bench.

Even though he knows he will use a tool again five minutes later, he never lays it down on the bench when he is temporarily finished with it: he puts it back in its permanent place on the wall tool rack. When he needs it again, he knows exactly where to find it. He doesn't have to paw through layers of other tools, scraps of wood, sandpaper, and miscellaneous junk to look for it. In fact, he hardly needs to look at all: he can reach almost without looking, like a typist using the touch system. His bench is bare, ready to be used as a bench is supposed to be used: a place to do work. It is not a storage shed.

A desk should be treated the same way: it is a place to do work, not to store things. The files and papers to be worked on should be brought to the desk as they are used, and then put away when not in use. Even if a file is going to be brought out again a half hour later, it is safer to take if off the desk in the meanwhile and put it into at least a semipermanent resting place. Not only will it be there when it is next needed, but there will be less danger of other, unrelated pieces of paper getting mixed up with that file and getting buried under its contents.

To make that practice work, you need to add another lesson that I learned from a superb executive: when he picked up a piece of paper off his morning inbound stack, he never laid it down until he had made some specific disposition of it. If it was a proposal that he was prepared to act on, he did it: "approved," "disapproved," whatever. If it called for a longer reply, he dictated it. If it was something more complicated, on which he could not act without more facts, more discussion—or even more thought of his own—he would define and schedule that: send it back to its source with a specific request for facts, schedule a meeting for discussion, or send it to his secretary to be brought back on a specific date. Meanwhile he made a note of what he wanted to weigh and consider. But off his desk went the paper.

Part of paper-shuffle trouble has nothing to do with paper as such: it is indecision—like putting off a decision that might displease or disappoint the writer of a letter. He has asked you to make a speech or serve on a committee or help his son-in-law get a job. Remember that he won't be any happier if he doesn't hear from you—because you set the letter aside to "think about it" and three weeks later it is still buried under the pile. He would be less unhappy with you if you had given him the bad news sooner and let him get started down another path. Anything would be better than your indecision.

Getting paper off your desk is bound to shift part of the burden to your secretary. But organizing files and followup systems is part of a secretary's professional job; and if you and she work out the system together, you will do her a favor by putting more order and sense into her program.

In our grandparents' time, the copy-book maxim was "a place for everything and everything in its place." That may sound so stiffly regimented as to leave no room for imagination or creativity. But it need not be so. The productive people of the world have used both the left hemisphere of the brain—the orderly, logical, linear side—and the right hemisphere—the more free-wheeling, imaginative side. The goal should be to harness the two together: in effect, to make the left hemisphere the servant of the right; to make it the doer that organizes and executes the bright ideas that are dreamed up by the less structured right side.

So the discipline that organizes the paperwork and office routine should not let that discipline be an end in itself; that stifles all initiative. Whether at the lowest clerical level or at the top of the executive pyramid, the purpose of order and organization is to help to get things done with the minimum of strain. If people are constantly buried in confusion, hunting for papers or scrambling to catch up with an unrecorded appointment, not only is less work done, but tempers begin to be raw and dispositions frayed and irritable.

Harnessing That Paper

Q While your advice to the executive was great, what suggestions do you have for the secretary on how to file this mound of paperwork? Also, a number of people refer to our files frequently; so I would like to have a system that is simple but with some kind of control.

A Even though I am addressing this to you, in answer to your question, I hope that your boss—and other bosses—will read this too; because they should understand that what you do is a large part of their success or failure in winning the paper chase.

They need to understand, too, that paperwork is more than just a necessary nuisance, and much more than just a clerical chore that they would consider beneath them. Management is an information business; and while more and more information is being stored, retrieved, and transmitted electronically, paper is still carrying the burden. It has to be managed, not left to chance.

If the executives in your office don't understand or appreciate those elements, maybe this one will grab them: with the rental cost of office space pushing up past $15 per square foot annually, to $20 and now as much as $25 in new buildings, the space devoted just to file cabinets, let alone all the mechanics of filing and paper handling, becomes a substantial item of cost. No one can afford to be careless in the use of space for any purpose; and the paper mill can push out the walls endlessly if it is not managed.

Add that to the payroll cost of all the people who handle the paper and you still don't have the biggest potential cost drain: the time loss of executives who have to wait if retrieval systems don't produce files quickly when needed.

The mountains of paper that every office has to generate—and keep—because of government requirements of record keeping and reporting create such a paper-handling problem that many companies just give up in despair at any thought of keeping the cost down. That is a mistake. This burden only makes it more important than ever, instead of rolling over and playing dead, to control everything that can be controlled—including the excesses caused by government.

Every company—and every office in it—has its own special requirements, and its system has to be adapted and tailored to meet those needs. But every system that works has a few of the same ingredients: it has a plan of organization, so that there is a logic as to where things should go, and where to look for them when they are needed again, plus a way of deciding which things should be kept, and for how long. You have added an extra ingredient, not always involved: the need for control because other people have access to the files.

Ideally, in such a situation, there would be a separate full-time file clerk or staff who would have exclusive control of everything that goes into or out of the files. If the volume does not justify that, I still would designate one person to be responsible and would require all others to check files in and out through that person.

If you are that one designated person—and I suspect from your letter that you are—then I would add only one more bit of advice on the mechanics of control: use an "out card" to show what has been removed, when, and by whom.

Meanwhile, every manager and his secretary should ask the same set of questions—the answers will form the basis of their system:

> What do we need to keep at all—and for how long?
>
> How can we find it and use it most easily—arranged by departments, by projects, or by other subject headings and groupings?
>
> How much do we want to break what we keep down into subsections, so that when we want to see some of it, we don't have to paw through seven other subjects to find what we want?
>
> Which pieces will we need to refer to most often?

Some of the answers are dictated by legal requirements or exposures. If your boss serves on one or more boards of directors, prudence will require that he retain certain records and materials that he might otherwise discard. He should consult his legal counsel as to what those items are, and for how long he should keep them.

How to lay out the system?

In a few offices, where there is only one kind of thing to file—trust accounts in a trust department, insurance policies in an

insurance office, investment accounts in an investment office—
an alphabetical file is the right way to go. But for most others,
an alphabetical system is a trap. It tends to develop a big fat
file under "M" for "Miscellaneous," and no one knows where to
put—or find—anything.

The way the files are organized should be an exact reflection of
the way your boss operates: the activities he supervises; the
reports he receives from others, the reports he must make to
others, together with the related correspondence; the support-
ing and related data he must follow; his interdepartmental and
other activities as part of general management, etc. His community, professional, and other extracurricular activities would
need a similar pattern. Then his personal files, instead of being
one big thick folder, should also be broken down into their
major categories, such as "Taxes," "Investments," "Insurance," "Health," etc.

You can be alphabetical within each subject-matter category,
but that is quite different from building the whole system
alphabetically.

The advantages of having on paper a full outline of the filing
plan are many: it is easier for you and your boss to visualize the
logic of the plan if you can lay it out where it can all be seen as a
connected whole. If he can say, "Yes, this is the way I work and
these are the things I need to keep handy," he is also likely to
be able to say, "This is fine, but we've overlooked so-and-so"; or
even more likely, "We need to break this one up into sections."

It is appalling how quickly the file drawers become obese with
paper that need not be kept at all. If the boss belongs to the
typical service club, trade association, or professional society,
and in addition serves on one or more civic boards and committees, he will get a steady stream of meeting notices and invitations—followed by minutes, committee reports, annual reports,

and project documents. You and he should agree on a strategy: for example, a file where you keep only the materials for the next upcoming meeting, so you and he can know where and when the meeting will be and what is coming up. But when that meeting is over and the next notice arrives, chuck the old stuff.

Unless the boss is currently active in the affairs of each organization, question whether you need to retain minutes or reports at all after he has read them. Even when he is active on a project and must keep everything until the project (or his service) is completed, could his files then be sent to the organization office and consolidated with theirs?

Once you and the boss have agreed, category by category, on what is to be kept and for how long, you should set up a retention-destruction schedule. I suggest you keep it in two forms: first, a master calendar that will tell you at a glance what is to be retained for a month, a quarter, a year, three years, or whatever; second, the same instruction marked on each file.

Whether you have a day or days each month when you do all the purging or do it piecemeal as each file reaches its "age limit" depends on the volume and on your own work habits. I lean toward designated days so that systematic emptying of files takes equal importance with putting things there in the first place. You need designated days for the inactive, closed file that still has to be kept for some number of years. If you don't have a schedule, it will still be there clogging your file a year or three after it should be dumped.

A central filing system serving many departments or sections and big enough to justify a full-time file clerk or staff is a different animal—same breed, but of different size and scope, and needing different controls. What makes it harder when you are doing your own filing is that you have so many other duties competing for your time. But remind your boss that it is in his interest, for his effectiveness, that you keep all files and paper-handling systems current and lean enough that you will always be able to retrieve just what he needs without keeping him waiting. To do that, you will have to set aside the necessary time.

Most of the current literature is not directly aimed at your problem. An excellent book, *Managing the Paperwork Pipeline* by Monroe S. Kuttner (John Wiley & Sons), bypasses much of your problem because it deals with so many other kinds of paperwork—the processing of purchase orders, etc.—and also because it places so much emphasis on electronic data-processing equipment and procedures. Even so, you might find it a helpful source of ideas. Remington Rand publishes a series of brochures all aimed at the sale of its various lines of equipment; one of these, *How to Unboggle Your Records Storage and Retrieval System,* has some useful suggestions. A chapter on modern filing systems in *Modern Archives,* by T. R. Schellenberg (University of Chicago Press) is pertinent.

Hidden Cost of Copies

Q Our biggest management problem is the skyrocketing cost of the Xerox machine. Our employees are running wild in their use of these copiers. Can you suggest ways to control that?

A I *could* say that if that is your biggest problem, you're lucky. But the fact is that you may have a bigger problem right there than you are facing up to: if you are just worrying about what you are paying for those photocopies, you are only looking at the tip of the iceberg. The hidden costs may be many times as great as that surface cost.

The simplest of the hidden costs is the time spent by everyone who has to read those copies. One of the curses of modern management is the mountain of paper that has to be waded through every day; and if these Xerox copies add unnecessarily to that burden, they add a double cost load: they use up time that has a real money value, and they postpone the time when the executive involved can get on to more productive work.

(A word of caution in the other direction: some of us who have worked in the field of communication have realized that one of the most common failures of internal communications in a company is the simple failure to send copies of certain key correspondence or policy decisions to appropriate people who had the "right to know." We tailored homely little devices like requiring secretaries always to ask, "Who else should get copies?" So the answer is not to go overboard in outlawing all copies, but to be more selective.)

The really big cost, though, is more deep-seated. Once a company starts a pattern of large-scale exchanging of copies, something else is likely to start to operate: the bureaucracy may begin to ask for comment, or action—or reaction—to whatever is in those copies. And before you know it, you have a Parkinsonian cluster of little cells around the company making studies or writing reports in response to what has appeared in the copies.

Even in a lean and healthy company, one transaction with the outside world—say, an order—triggers twenty-five or thirty transactions inside the company. Once Xerox Parkinsonism gets going, that ratio can rise fast. One observer estimates, in extreme cases, as many as 135 internal transactions for every external action.

So look behind the paper mill and see how much busywork—makework—has been created that is not really adding anything to your earnings. It may indeed be a serious drain on your earnings, if only because it is slowing down the profit-making output.

In all of this, remember the old World War II question "Is this trip necessary?" and paraphrase it to read "Is this trip to the Xerox machine necessary?" The real issue, though, is, "Is this *copy* necessary?"

(Incidentally, the Xerox machine has almost replaced the water cooler and the coffee machine as a gathering place for gossip. And it tops either of the other two shrines as an excuse to get away from the boredom of other work—especially if the copier is on a different floor or in a distant room: "I'll be gone for a while—I've got to go photocopy something.")

II

Hiring Good People

While the management of himself is the first thing an executive has to do, his job obviously doesn't end there —that is only the beginning.

The work of his company has to be done by other people. So his next concern has to be the hiring of good people; then the training—and the retraining—of those good people. That in turn leads to all the things that help to keep people, and keep them effective.

Don't Rush
Personnel Decisions

Q My company has 1,800 employees and we are growing steadily. We are having to expand our executive and supervisory organization as well as our general workforce. That growth is causing me to make decisions that I am not used to making—decisions about how to structure and staff the new jobs. Should we promote entirely from within, or should we go outside to fill many of the new jobs? Our internal choices are not ideal in a few cases, and even though it takes time to search outside, some of my associates are pressuring me to move faster. It's time, they say, that I had a full crew on.

A Tell your associates to keep their shirts on—but help them to understand why. In most areas of corporate action, decisions can be made relatively fast. The one area where it pays to take your time—not to dawdle or procrastinate, but to be thorough—is in the selection of key people. Errors of judgment in other business areas can be costly, but can be survived if the batting average—the ratio of good to bad judgment—is high.

But a mistake in the picking of an executive can be devastating.

One other caution: while the final decision may be yours, you should not hesitate—in fact, you must not *fail*—to get inputs from others in appropriate places and at appropriate levels. Any one person's evaluation of a candidate—including your own—will inevitably reflect some degree of bias. You should offset the effect of that bias by getting it out where you can look at it. You balance your bias against the appraisals of others—who also have biases, but different ones.

Basic to selection of people, of course, is another kind of discipline: you must define what you need in each job. Your job description should suggest the qualities, characteristics, experience, and abilities that will be needed. You are looking for a good man or good woman—but good for what? You know the old story about the man who met his friend on the street and inquired, "How's your wife?" The friend replied, "Compared with what?"

That remark suggests another caution about the selection process: comparison. A wise friend of mine, a highly effective president of a large university, had a standard question that he put to any dean who came to him with a recommendation for a new appointment to the faculty. After reviewing and analyzing all the other credentials of the candidate, the president would ask the dean, "What others did you consider and turn down?"

An occasional dean had, like many a corporate executive, considered only one prospect. He had simply advanced a favorite, or someone with whom he had become infatuated. That kind of automatic grab sometimes worked; it is possible, once in a great while, to pick up a "sleeper" that way.

But even in such lucky exceptions, something had been missed. If the recommended candidate had the most impeccable, unchallengeable credentials, the comparison with others helped to put his qualifications on a scale, to be weighed against the norms of the field and of the market. Not only was the choice right, but everyone knew it was right.

No two candidates will look alike in the profile of their qualifications. Few if any will add up to perfection on any objective scale. That's why it is so important to measure each one against the requirements of the particular job. Is he strong where you need strengths? Are his deficiences ones you can live with?

Especially if you are leaning toward one candidate but not feeling comfortable about him, you should ask yourself why not.

You should neither shut your eyes and grab for one who gives you that vague feeling of concern and uneasiness nor turn him down just on that account. Probe your own feelings deeper by checking him out, point by point, against your specification sheet.

You are sure to find that he is weak somewhere, in some one of the areas you have specified on that sheet. You can now judge whether the weakness is crucial. If he's weak on one of the key requirements, he's not likely to succeed at the job. So stop wasting your time and look for someone else. But if the flaw is only mildly troubling, a weak spot you can build around, then stop being troubled about him.

Don't necessarily pick him—but go back to your "compared with what" test and see if he is the best talent available in the market.

You ask whether you should promote entirely from within, or should go outside to fill many jobs. There is no single, simple answer, but there are some guidelines:

If you have always hired the right kind of people at the lower levels and have always done the right kind of development, so that you have the right person ready for every vacancy, of course you should promote from within. To do otherwise would be deadly to morale, and to your chances of continuing to hire and retain good people.

But because the world seldom operates so perfectly, you will occasionally have openings for which no one inside is right for the job. Then you should not hesitate to go outside. You want the best people for each job, and to compromise on that one is to start down the road to mediocrity.

If your company is growing as fast as you say and expanding your executive organization in proportion, you may be creating positions for which there could have been no preparation; and you may have no choice but to go outside.

But the principles remain the same and you should examine inside candidates before you close that door.

Here's one other suggestion that won't help you make your choice but may make it easier to live with: after you have made your decision but before you have announced it, take the extra time to tell each of the unsuccessful candidates that you had to pick someone else this time. Don't let them read it in the paper or hear it for the first time from someone else.

And if you have been consulting with others (as I hope you have), give them the courtesy of telling them if you are not following their advice. You'll have other heads to hunt, and a reputation for wise recruiting is an essential mark of the good executive.

Ingredients for Success

Q Which quality in a young person do you consider the most important single ingredient for success?

A You probably expect me to say "intelligence" or "moral acter." Neither is the answer. You have to expect him to have at least average or better than average intelligence; and if there is any question about his honesty, integrity, or morals, you don't want him around at all. But the highest marks in either or both of those will not be a guarantee of success. Every company of any size has employees of superior IQ and sterling morals who never got out of the starting gate.

No, my nomination for single most important ingredient is *energy well directed.* The person with a good sense of direction, who knows what the goals and game plan of the company are, who judges every idea and every action in terms of its contribution to that plan—and then works energetically and persistently to perfect and complete those ideas and actions—is going to be the winner. He has to have those other qualities to qualify at all; but this is the one that will put him ahead.

I know that others who have written on this subject have suggested still other qualities they consider equally or more important. Most often mentioned is "the ability to work effectively"
(or "harmoniously") "with other people."

I must agree that this one deserves a very high place in any
such list. In the absence of any offsetting negatives, it will virtually guarantee progress a considerable distance up the ladder. But just as a relative matter, it has not seemed as sure a
prescription for reaching the very top as the sense of direction,
or "focus," that I had mentioned.

On the negative side, certainly nothing will *prevent* progress
more—nothing is a surer prescription for failure—than the in-
ability to work effectively with other people.

Since there is nothing incompatible about the two qualities,
why settle for less than the best? Look for both.

Returning Prodigal

Q A man we had considered a real "comer" in our company left us three years ago to go to what looked like a better job. Now he wants to come back and we really could use him. But I'm afraid of what it will do to the morale of our organization. We have a policy of never rehiring anyone who left; if we abandon that policy, will we be encouraging others to leave us? And will even those who don't leave us be resentful?

A That depends on how you handle the returning prodigal. If you kill a fatted calf for him, expect some unhappy reactions from those who stayed with you. But you don't have to do it that way.

Before we talk about how you treat these people, let's talk about your policy itself. There is nothing wrong with it: many fine companies have had a similar policy and still adhere to it. But there also is nothing sacred about it: policies can be revised when conditions justify a change, and many other fine companies have moved away from hard-and-fast policies against rehiring. Today's greater mobility, with more executives and especially technical specialists moving from company to company, has changed many of the traditional attitudes between companies and their employees. For better or for worse, the paternal relationship that implied that employees "belonged" to the company has been gradually replaced by more of a professional-and-client relationship.

That does not suggest that you toss all your old policies out the window and adopt an open-door, come-and-go-as-you-please attitude. Far from it. You should remain entirely selective.

And while you might well modify your stance enough that the door is no longer slammed shut and forever locked to the departing associate, the one thing everyone should understand—if you want to avoid later grief—is that no one who leaves can expect to come back to the same job he or she left. That job is going to be filled, and no one should be dislodged from it to make room for the returnee.

The ideal way to fit a returnee back into the organization is to find an assignment for him that is not in the direct line of traditional promotion. *Any* job is likely to have aspirants who would like to move into it; but that is certain with a job that is in the vertical line of climb. So even if it is not his old job, there will be resentment if he fills one that someone just below could expect to fill. And it is not only the immediate disappointed candidate whose nose will be out of joint: everyone below him who might have moved up a notch will be equally sprained.

So where do you put the prodigal son or daughter? Look for the unstructured spot, off the organization chart—a special assignment, if possible, that has no precedent and in which no one else can feel any vested interest. If you are considering an acquisition, you might use this person to make studies of various aspects of the transaction: not only the orthodox economic and financial appraisals, but such special facets as how people in the two companies are to match up—a touchy subject for the in-house regulars to handle.

Or you may have a situation where you can send him right into some newly acquired property, either to take charge or to represent your interest in a transition (especially if this is in a line of business that is new to you so that none of your regulars would be natural choices for the assignment).

The ideal situation is one that no one else would want because it would be a sidetracking from normal progression. Here is an example: You are about to build a new headquarters office building, perhaps as a joint venture with another invenstor. You need someone to represent your interest in bird-dogging the project. He doesn't have to be an engineer or construction expert, but he has to have good broad-based business sense; and he has to have both the sense to know when he needs specialized help and the maturity to be unafraid to bring in that help. Ambitious mainstreamers who would qualify for this assignment might feel that they were being sent to Siberia if they were taken off their present jobs, because this building project is, in itself, a dead end; but it is made to order for the returnee: he doesn't compete with the mainstreamers, but he will be in enough contact with them that by the time the job is finished he again will be an "old-timer."

When you say "we really could use him," it sounds as though your company is growing. So you should have many such special spots in which to farm a returnee out for a year or two—long enough for him to reestablish himself, so that the next time you want to consider him for a competitive appointment, he will not be thought of as a returnee, but as a regular who has earned the appointment on his merits.

Incidentally, such a farm-out can give you a chance to test him in some new roles, and to see if he has even more potential than you had realized before.

Hiring the Handicapped

Q We have had no job applications from handicapped persons, nor any outside pressure to hire anyone who is handicapped. But I am aware that there are organized movements on behalf of the handicapped, and I am wondering how I should respond if they come to my door.

A Because it is not the purpose of this column to deal with social issues, I shall not dwell on the purely humane aspects of the problem; but I could otherwise give you a lengthy lecture in support of the objectives of these organized efforts, stating that those with physical handicaps, just like those whose race, color, sex, or religion had formerly been a social and economic handicap, should be helped to participate as fully in the economic life of society as their individual talents and potential abilities will permit, with no arbitrary barriers placed in their way.

Since my job is to help managers manage more effectively, I shall instead focus on how you can best manage this part of your job.

One of the two top priorities of the CEO is to see that the best possible people are in every spot in the company. He selects for the top spots himself, and he should make sure that the personnel machinery is geared to putting the right people in place all down the line.

That means that the company should not cut itself off from any promising source of supply—and the field of the handicapped is one of those sources.

In fact, some of those who have been drawing on it have begun to think that this may be the greatest untapped source of good personnel.

Not every handicapped person is capable of filling every open job, but neither is every nonhandicapped. Selection and placement are just as important in the one case as in the other—probably even more important with the handicapped, because there are even more reasons for trying to avoid failure. But the selection process should be without prejudice.

And let's be blunt about it: there has been prejudice among employers against hiring the handicapped. Like many such prejudices, it has been based on fear and apprehension: fear of accidents, fear of costly errors, fear that company supervisors might not be able to handle all the problems that are visualized, fear that other employees might be uncomfortable working with the handicapped, fear that customers might react badly, etc., etc. Like many such fears, these have tended to evaporate in the face of actual experience. What was feared just didn't happen.

Employers in many different fields have reported successful experience in employing persons with disabilities—not only huge companies like Sears Roebuck, IBM, Metropolitan Life, and Du Pont, but much smaller ones as well. Even before handicapped persons were brought under affirmative-action requirements, some of these companies had developed innovative programs of their own. (Incidentally, I assume that you have checked with your legal department as to whether you are subject to those requirements. The rest of what I am saying applies equally whether you are or not.)

What these companies have found is that the job performance is at least as good, on average, as that of the nonhandicapped and in some cases better; and that the experience with turnover and absenteeism has been at least as good and sometimes better. Part of the reason for the performance record is better training and supervision; the very nature of the job assignment—the use of the mentally retarded, for example—has called for a different approach to training, but it has paid off.

Part of the reason why such problems as turnover and absenteeism have been minimized lies in something that is not inherent in the nature of the handicapped person, but has developed as a plus outside the place of employment: all across America there are community organizations set up to help the handicapped gain employment. While much of the activity of these organizations is pointed toward persuading employers to hire the handicapped, another purpose is to counsel and guide these persons themselves, to help prepare them to make their employment a success.

Generally speaking, these community organizations can be an additional resource to you in helping you resolve questions about how to deal with unusual situations.

The companies that have moved extensively into the hiring of the handicapped have, of course, had to prepare their supervisors to be cooperative, if only because the program would require a variety of physical and other accommodations. Many had expected to meet much more resistance than they did. As for the attitudes of other employees, companies have reported that morale actually improved in the units where handicapped workers were introduced. The feeling of a "family" and a "team" was reported.

Customers generally seem to have reacted very well—at least wherever the placement has taken customer convenience into account. For example, a woman in a wheelchair has been made manager of a branch bank in California and has been well received by her customers—who find that loan decisions can be made just as well from a wheelchair as from a swivel chair.

Do You Need an M.B.A.?

Q I see that most big corporations, and many medium-size ones like mine, actively recruit M.B.A.s as they graduate from business schools. We have never done that, nor have we hired any M.B.A.s. Are we missing something, or is this just another fad, like thinking you must have an IBM 3033 system whether you need it or not?

A There is no doubt that things like hiring M.B.A.s and installing big computer systems can become gimmicks and status symbols; but it is also true that M.B.A.s, like computers, have filled a real need.

You put your finger close to the central question when you say "whether you need it or not." The question is not just whether you need M.B.A.s, but why, and to do what. What advantage does hiring an M.B.A. bring you? How do you propose to use that extra ingredient? Do benefits justify the cost?

First, let's get clear just what you do and don't get in hiring an M.B.A. There is nothing about that degree that automatically guarantees success. There is virtually nothing that a graduate student learns in those two years of study that he or she could not learn, sooner or later, without taking that degree. So then what is the point of it?

Part of the point is in those words "sooner or later." The graduate arrives on the job with at least a minimum basic grounding in such things as business accounting, economics, financial analysis, investment analysis, and the uses of and return on capital. It might take him five years to learn all of this on the job, if indeed he can be exposed to it all.

Meanwhile he can approach every assignment with a sharper awareness of how that transaction will impact on the company's whole business plan. In fact, the very concept of a "business plan" is something that might take him a long time to pick up just from this job exposure, but it would be one of the first things an M.B.A. would try to identify.

There is a related advantage. Because the M.B.A. is introduced to all of these basic business tools in a relatively short time and because they are presented in the context of business administration, the M.B.A. is more likely to focus on them as tools of business planning, not as mere vocational skills. It is a different kind of perspective.

Having spelled out these pluses, we still have the question, Why do you want an M.B.A.?

Most business schools have majors-within-major, so that the graduates come out specializing in finance or investment or marketing or accounting. If you need to upgrade your competence in one of these fields, look for candidates who have taken more than the minimum of work in that area. It's also a good idea to look for candidates from schools that are known to have strong programs in that particular field.

Which leads to another caveat: you don't have to compete with the biggest recruiters for the product of the three or four top-rated business schools. If you know what you want and where to look for it, you can profitably do some shopping in some of the other excellent but less prestigious schools.

This may be a propitious time for that kind of shopping; there is some evidence that we may now have a "buyer's market"—that the supply of M.B.A.s may exceed the demand.

Even so, when you embark on this kind of hiring program, you are introducing new elements into your entire compensation and personnel administration. You must be prepared to deal with the repercussions. The cost, weighed against the benefits, involves more than just the differential in starting pay, which in itself is not necessarily a disruptive factor if it is handled wisely. The less visible costs are the greater ones: your own time and that of all your executives and supervisors.

Luncheon Faux Pas

Q You have talked about using the expense-account lunch to get better acquainted with customers and others with whom you do business. But you didn't mention another use of the business lunch: to size up someone you are thinking of hiring. A *New York Times* article recently recommended taking a candidate for a senior position to lunch and watching how he handles himself—what wine he orders, his eye and body movements when certain subjects are mentioned, his table manners when put under sudden pressure, what he reveals about his home life and other personal history, etc. Do you think that kind of observing is a reliable way to judge a prospective executive, and does it tell you what you really want to know?

A It may tell as much about you as it does about your candidate: what your values are and what you think are important characteristics. It may also depend on how skilled you are in seeing through superficial behavior. I am not an authority on body language, but I suspect that many of the people you might be considering would be sophisticated enough

49

themselves to guard against many tell-tale faux pas or mannerisms.

A man who later became chief executive of one of America's largest chemical companies once told me that when he was head of the company's research department he used to use a luncheon visit as a setting to apply one final screening test when he was considering a young chemist for a research position. After he had interviewed the candidate and reviewed his file to satisfy himself of his technical competence, he would take him to lunch. If the candidate reached for the salt before he had tasted his food, my friend never hired him. "He wasn't sufficiently interested in getting the facts first."

If you as employer are sure enough of your ground to stake your judgment on one such criterion, well and good.

In general, I would rather dig more deeply into a candidate's track record, as revealed through checking with other sources, than to depend too heavily on this kind of game playing. But I would not dismiss entirely the value of the luncheon visit as an additional evaluating process. The more informal setting, away from your office, does of course offer the possibility that you will learn something about the candidate's history that did not show up in the formal application or headhunter's report.

And whether you play gamesmanship or not, you are entitled to take a general "intuitive" kind of reading on how you feel about the candidate. While you should not act impulsively to accept or reject a candidate just on the basis of those feelings, you still should take heed of them if only as a signal that you should check further if something bothers you.

"Cutting Costs, Cutting People"

Q We are in the midst of a cost-cutting campaign, which I can't criticize because I ordered it myself; but I am having a bad time with my expense-control task force about some of the places they want to cut.

For example, they want to cut deeply in most of the places where we meet the public, including customers. I don't mean the salesmen—they are pretty much on a commission or incentive basis—but the service departments, complaint or return desks, receptionists, even the order desks.

The cost cutters not only want to cut back on the numbers in these sections, but to lower their grades so we would use lower-salaried people; they imply that "anybody can do those jobs—you don't need as high a level of personnel as you are using now."

I don't agree. Do you?

A Your task force may be right on the numbers. Only by measuring the volume of work done can you answer that; and if these service people are not using all their time productively, you may have a choice between reducing their numbers and adding to their duties (assuming that there are other tasks they could handle in their idle time).

But be careful about lowering the grades and thereby getting inferior people on these sensitive jobs—whether inferior either in their native ability or in training and experience.

In the first place, by cutting down on quality, you may defeat your hope of cutting down on numbers. It has been demonstrated that good people are the cheapest in the long run: the superior people will outperform the mediocre ones, not by a margin of 10 or 20%, but by as much as 200 or 300%. Of course the superior performers expect to be paid more than those who are run of the mill; but you can do that and still be money ahead. At every level—clerical, supervisory, middle management, or senior management—the cost per unit of acceptable output is less if you have good people.

But there is a catch in this: it won't work unless all the supervisory people are able, and willing, to do their part of the job. They have to do the laborious screening to get the superior people in the first place; then they have to follow through to see that they continue to get superior performance.

That is hard work; and you need supervisors who know quality performance when they see it, who know the difference between high-standard and shoddy performers. That isn't as simple as it might sound.

There is another reason, though, why you should be cautious about making arbitrary cuts in the particular areas you mention as targets of your task force's meat ax. These are among the most sensitive spots in any company. They are the front line of contact with a large part of sales volume, including a special segment of your customers: the ones who have problems or special needs or special demands. How they are treated when they come to your service personnel can color their attitude toward your whole company and your products.

Even those customers who have no such special needs are still potential trouble spots for you. The purchasing agent who is about to place the most routine order usually has other competitive sources that could supply what he wants. If his telephone inquiry about price or delivery meets with a surly or lackadaisical response—with anything but the most crisply competent and cooperative response—he may just drop you and move on to another supplier. Especially if it happens to him more than once, he may well conclude that if the people on the order desk are as sloppy as that, he cannot count on the other departments doing any better about getting his order delivered on time.

What Price Personnel?

Q The cost of our personnel department has been going up, up, up for the past several years. I'm wondering whether we're getting our money's worth out of it, and whether we couldn't get along without most of what they do?

A You should raise those questions from time to time about everything that goes on in your company. But don't be in a hurry to dump any of your personnel function overboard *just* because its cost is going up. Try to get better performance for less money, of course; but also look at what you are getting for your money.

Until recently most CEOs have thought that personnel work could not be measured or evaluated quantitatively—partially because personnel managers themselves haven't known how to measure their performance. And many of them haven't wanted to learn. But that is changing, as they have had to face that no function can be divorced from its relation to the bottom line—and personnel is no exception.

Happily, as personnel people have begun to look more critically at the cost-benefit effectiveness of their work, they have found that when the personnel operation is properly viewed and properly performed, they do not have to be defensive about it, but can feel pride in its contribution to earnings.

An appalling part of what has skyrocketed personnel costs in recent years, of course, is something that neither personnel nor top management ever asked for but that inescapably fell to personnel departments to handle. It is the whole area of compliance with expanding government regulations—EEO, ERISA, OSHA, and the like.

Here the problem of measuring cost is complicated by the fact that personnel shares responsibility with other parts of the company, both operating units and staff services like legal. Better yardsticks for measuring and allocating costs will evolve with experience, but meanwhile you can ask yourself two questions that almost answer themselves, even if inexactly: first, what would it save if no one in the company monitored compliance? One severe penalty for noncompliance could outweigh the entire cost of your personnel department. Second, what would it save if compliance were taken away from personnel and disbursed throughout the company, with every unit responsible for its own? Aside from the fact that at least as many man-hours would probably be spent on the activity, with no assurance that the people involved would be well versed in what they should be doing, the greatest cost to the bottom line would be that every minute spent on this peripheral activity would be a distraction from the main business of the unit—to make, sell, or deliver a product or service.

But the compliance function, burdening and demanding as it is on the personnel department, is not the central reason for its being. That central reason is to help top management make sure that the right numbers of the right kinds of people are hired, are properly trained to do their jobs, and are so treated that the best ones will remain with the company, and that as people are needed to fill successively higher levels of administration and management, the right ones will have had the necessary preparation for that succession.

Every part of that central function can be evaluated, and most of it in hard numbers. Some of those numbers, in themselves, provide a clue to the importance of the personnel function. Take the sheer, bare-bones cost of hiring: it can be measured and pinpointed as to source of applicants, level of position filled, and other characteristics. When it is seen that the cost per hire can range from a few hundred to several thousand dollars, this activity alone assumes some bottom-line importance. But that is only the beginning. Adding in the costs of training, indoctrination, and supervision produces a figure for the direct dollar cost of turnover. Even that is not the whole story: less quantifiable but equally observable is the disruptive effect on productivity when turnover is high. And while turnover is a resultant of many forces in a company, it is the role of a personnel department to guide other departments, and top management itself, in directions that will hold turnover to a minimum.

All this, of course, is personnel functioning at its best, and not all personnel departments do function at their best. You are entitled to know whether yours does; and now that the techniques for evaluating and measuring are improving, you have the possibility of comparing the performance of your department with those in other companies. Not only that, but you can better compare the performance of individuals within the department.

The literature on this subject, while not large, is growing. Some trade associations have made and published studies in this field. The American Bankers Association, for example, commissioned a study by Booz, Allen & Hamilton, Inc., that is right on target: published under the title *Measuring the Effectiveness of the Personnel Function,* it discusses the need for, and presents a model of, a personnel function evaluation system, called the Personnel Planning and Evaluation System (PAES). The American Management Association and the Conference Board also have some good material within their publications.

III

Developing the People

Once you have picked the best people you can find, and have given them the best training and preparation for their present and future jobs, you not only have a big investment in those people, but you have an asset that needs to be protected.

If you treat them only as figures on the balance sheet, they can slip away from you, and wipe out even those balance-sheet figures. They must be treated as human beings, with human needs, aspirations, and desires—as much in their last days on the job as in their first. If they are not, their last days may follow their first sooner than you had expected.

Part of what is involved is a companywide concern, and will be dealt with in Part IX, concerned with morale. But part of it involves individual situations that must be dealt with one by one, on a case-by-case basis. Compensation is part of it, but only a part.

Reasonable Compensation

Q Is there available information on the range, in dollars, that owner-executives may pay themselves without fear of challenge by the tax authorities? We fully understand that the burden of proof is on the taxpayer; but there should be ranges or guidelines. This is a real problem for the small closely held business.

A First let me make one thing clear: I do not give tax advice. Your own tax adviser should give you the final word on the tax aspects of your problem. But you can help him—and yourself—by being sure you have done your own homework.

The general rule—the "buzzword"—of the tax fraternity is "reasonable compensation." That means that if your company wants to be able to treat your salary as a deductible expense, and not a dividend, and if you want to treat it as earned income, instead of dividend, it must be reasonable. But that is a question of fact; and the test is what you would command as pay if you were employed in a more competitive atmosphere where you could not set your own salary.

Since the tax examiners and courts will look for hard evidence, you should look for the same kind of evidence. They will ask, "What does an individual receive who performs similar duties in a similar situation?" And what they will try to find "evidentially" is a comparable job not only in a similar industry, but in a company of comparable size. They will also look at the relationship between your salary and the profitability of your company; if it is a high percentage, that would raise a negative signal flag and put more burden of proof on you. Again the tax authorities would compare your ratio with others in the same industry.

While they are looking, they also will look at the salary history of any individual in the company who is part of the close group who set their own pay. If he worked elsewhere at a comparable job before he came into this one, was his pay comparable—or has it been jumped 'way up?

Most of the comparisons except this last, personal one can be checked out from industrywide sources. Since you would have the burden of proof if you were challenged, you might as well do your own checking in advance to satisfy yourself that you and your associates are acting "reasonably."

You will find comparisons in broad general categories of business and industry in the publication of the Conference Board, *Top Executive Compensation;* and in *Executive Compensation Service,* published by the American Management Association. Both are in New York City. The Conference Board also publishes, in alternate years, *Directors' Compensation;* since that also is potentially a tax issue in closely held companies, you may want to check that. Nonmembers may purchase these publications but at a higher price than for members.

The Research Institute of America, with offices in New York, also does a periodic survey of compensation, as do Dartnell

Company in Chicago and the firm of Towers, Perrin, Forster and Crosby. Each of these covers a different segment of the field, which might or might not touch on your industry or bracket.

But after you have checked these general sources, you should consult your own trade association (or associations) to see if they have something much more pinpointed to your situation. Some trade associations have made most detailed surveys broken down not only by size of company but by minute function, such as "legal expense, as ratio of sales volume."

Bonus Babies

Q We have a family business, 50% owned by each of two brothers; one has three sons in the business, and the other has five. The question of compensation for extra effort—i.e., a bonus plan—is a knotty one. How do you set up a formula that is best for all, and fair over a period of years? Or is it impossible to do without wrecking the company and the futures of the third generation?

A If I thought your problem applied only to family or closely held companies, I might have decided not to deal with it here. But the issues are the same in any company that has bright and ambitious young people competing with each other. The issues get magnified when the Young Turks are in the same family; but that only makes the problem easier to examine with naked eyes.

It not only is *not* impossible to do without wrecking the company, but may be the only way to avoid damaging choices. When there are no incentives to reward excellence, either the company settles down into a sleepy lethargy, in which case the most able young people will get out, or those able ones, seeing more potential in the company, may stir up dissension in their effort to gain control and shake up the company.

So I favor an incentive plan—call it a bonus if you want—as part of the compensation package, *provided* it is a real incentive plan, not just added compensation under a fancy disguise. That means it meets these tests:

1. The participating officers and employees are not able to count on it year after year whether they perform or not; it should be granted when earned (or rather, *to the extent* earned) and withheld to the extent not earned.
2. Target bonus levels are set for participating positions so that, when combined with median salary values for the job, they produce a fully competitive total income.
3. The distribution under the plan is not left to the whims or discretion of someone or a few at the top, but is based on measurable performance toward specifically defined business objectives.
4. Everyone who will participate in the plan knows all its provisions, including any changes, by the beginning of the fiscal year covered by the plan.
5. While the objectives and the criteria to measure performance are set by management, they are communicated to participants in advance and accepted by them as understood, realistic, and achievable.
6. A separation is made between a management bonus plan, restricted to positions that can substantially affect the attainment of *overall* business goals, and a plan for those who have impact only on *functional* objectives.
7. A board committee dominated by outside directors (even in a family company, I hope you have some *really* outside directors!) makes final decisions on distributions to management-level positions, and approves the structure of the plan for all positions, including total amount

to be allocated to the plan, maximum ratio of bonus to base salary, number of positions to be included, business objectives to be included in the measurement, the relative weight to be given each, and the criteria to be used in the measurement.

Within those universal specifications, each company must tailor the details to fit the priorities of its own game plan. How many points to increased earnings per share vs. how many points to return on equity? How important is increased market share? Or accuracy in forecasting? What other contributions to business plans are important and can be measured?

Because the relative importance of these factors (and others you will introduce) will change over the years, I raise a caution— two cautions in opposite directions—over your point "fair over a period of years." You *will* find it necessary to reexamine your plan from time to time and make modifications. But—don't do it too often. Three years is a good rule of thumb as a testing period for each version. And *never* make an abrupt change in your plan just because market or other special conditions made the results too fat or too lean in one year. Keep your perspective focused on the long pull. And above all, don't tinker with the plan to favor or penalize any individual.

In your special case, if your eight "juniors" take part in setting your objectives, your weighting formula, and your measurement criteria, such a plan should help them to see, as much as any plan can, what relative roles and rewards they are "entitled" to.

For any other company, a properly constructed and administered incentive plan can help to separate the men from the boys—and the women from the girls.

Tried-and-True
vs. Gamble

Q We are exploring a new project that would associate a number of other companies with us in a joint enterprise, to offer a new kind of service across the country. The job of approaching and negotiating with these companies calls for a person with special skills and maturity. Our dilemma is whether to detach one of our promising younger executives, thereby interrupting his career for as much as a year or more, with no certainty that the project will ever materialize and lead to any new opportunities for him, or to take one of our tested older people, possibly someone at or near retirement, who could make this a final assignment or possibly even an extension of his active service.

Is there any experience that would guide us in our choice?

A One of the decisions an executive repeatedly has to make is how to balance his use of the talents of older, more seasoned employees with the energies and ambitions of the promising younger ones.

There is always the temptation to assign difficult, out-of-pattern projects to the "tried and true" veterans who have demonstrated that they know how to handle tough and unusual problems. There is even the temptation to give these assignments to those about to retire—to extend the period of service, making the retirement less abrupt.

These are the "safe" people, and this is the "safe" way to go. But there are dangers that make this less than totally safe.

The danger is not that the job will not be done well. That is the safe part. But more is at stake than just getting *that* job done well. There nearly always is more involved than the job at hand, and for the executive, every decision is likely to have at least two parts: the immediate results, and the effect on the longer-range strength and performance of the company.

Ideally, the two objectives will not be in conflict. But when they are, the executive must decide how much the tradeoffs are worth—how much immediate value should be sacrificed for how much longer-range benefit, or vice versa.

In the choice between veterans and those less experienced, the tradeoffs have a degree of gamble. The veterans *might* handle the immediate assignment better, but not necessarily: a highly motivated junior might do still better. Less of a gamble is that introducing the junior to a new experience and a new challenge will probably build his strengths, and therefore add to the company's supply of seasoned operators far more than having the veteran repeat familiar strategies and techniques.

How badly the wrong decision can backfire was demonstrated by an experience we had in our bank. As with most banks, our loans to business were mostly for shorter terms; companies that needed longer credits were expected to go to other sources—insurance companies or pension funds typically.

Our loan administrators came to realize that if we sent our borrowers out on the street to hunt up their own sources of long-term money, we lost some of the continuity of our contact with them—a precious asset to a multiservice bank.

So it was decided that we should ourselves seek to develop a working relationship with long-term lenders. Then when one of our customers needed longer-term credit than we could supply, we could work out a package in which we would take the shorter maturities and we would call upon one of the other institutions to supply the longer end.

To sell this idea required many months of negotiation—traveling back and forth across the country to meet and talk with the chief lending officers, and sometimes the loan committees, of these institutions.

The task seemed made to order for one of our most senior and most respected loan officers who was about to retire. He was glad to take it on, and he did it superbly.

But standing on the sidelines was a younger man, also with great ability. He was furious. Not only did he feel that the idea was his (he had not made any formal proposal, but had been the first one to suggest the idea informally during committee discussions), but he was sure that he could have handled the negotiations equally well, and that the experience would have been valuable to him in his later responsibilities.

Not long afterward he left the bank, saying that he didn't seem to be appreciated and wasn't being given a chance to use his abilities. He became a president of a smaller bank, which he led with distinction.

His leaving was a great shock to his colleagues and supervisors, who felt they had indeed appreciated him; in fact, they thought of him as one of their stars. But they had not shown it in the way that would have been most persuasive to him.

So the short-run results of this management decision were excellent. But the long-range results were a disaster.

None of this suggests that the older performers should be dumped or sidetracked as soon as vigorous new stars appear. Far from it. But their roles can be quite different.

The older and younger executives often can in fact work together. But they should do so in ways that do not block the growth of the younger ones. What the veterans should be able to contribute, out of their experience, is counsel and judgment—something the younger men can acquire only by their own direct involvement.

Wherever possible the younger ones should conduct or at least be involved in any negotiations that are part of the project. These not only build their acquaintance, but help to build their confidence in themselves. They should be part of the decision-making process, so that exercising judgment becomes, early in their careers, part of their equipment and habit pattern.

How Do You Treat
Older People Humanely?

Q We have a man who holds a key position in the management of one of our major departments—but doesn't fit in very well. He looked good when he first joined us eighteen years ago, but he has not grown and developed with the company.

Now we are wondering what we are going to do about him. He is blocking an important function; but he is fifty-seven years old. Are we stuck with him until normal retirement age?

A Remember that how you treat this man will be a signal to all the rest of your employees of how they can expect to be treated, especially as they grow older.

This man has been with you for eighteen years, and you say he is not performing up to your requirements. But I gather that he has not changed much—it is just that the job has gotten bigger and you expect more.

Apart from the fact that he is fifty-seven years old and will find it geometrically harder to find a new job than if you had acted five or ten years ago, you have an obligation that started at least that long ago. When a company keeps anyone on its payroll for ten years, it acquires an institutional obligation—not to keep him in a particular job if he is not adequate to that job, but an obligation to treat him humanely, not just "dump him out in the snow."

You knew—or should have known—as much about this man after ten years as you ever would know. Since you kept him nearly twice that long, I think you owe it to him either to find another slot in your company that he can handle effectively, without impeding the momentum of others; or to help him land on his feet somewhere—possibly through the outplacement process I describe elsewhere in this book.

IV

People for the Future

The demand on the executive is that he have people in place to fill present and *future* personnel needs.

Succession planning has its own special problems—but none so great as failing to plan.

Because it calls into play so many of the facets of the art of being an executive—especially his sense of perspective on where the company should be going and what it will take to get there—succession planning is singled out for separate examination.

Stand-ins Don't Stand Idle

Q You have said that companies and their executives are judged by the depth of management and the preparation for succession. How far down the ladder would you go with that? A company can't afford to have understudies or "stand-ins" waiting at everyone's elbow.

A Who said anything about standing or waiting? If you are going to use theatrical terms, let's remember that actors go on playing their own subordinate roles after they are trained and ready to step into the star's shoes. Executives and supervisors can do the same thing. So we're not talking about feather-bedding, or using two people to do one job. We're talking about acting like a repertory company, where there is always more than one person who knows the lines for each part and could step in in an emergency.

You open a good question, because not all the sensitive spots in a company are up near the top. In many companies, the loss of the CEO would disrupt the momentum of the operation less than to lose a key technician several layers down who has no

75

replacement. He might be a chemist or a market trader; but if he sits in daily control of some central part of the company's business flow, his absence could put a costly damper on output—which means on earnings.

Some jobs in a company are important to long-range planning but are not sensitive day to day. Examples: corporate and organization planning; systems and equipment research; and even the function that is called "long-range planning."

Others are vital to daily operation but involve service that is usually available in the market. Examples: janitorial and other building maintenance; electrical, plumbing, and other mechanical service and maintenance.

But all through your company you may have individuals with special skills or special know-how who cannot be replaced on a moments' notice, whose sudden removal from the scene would cause havoc—and for whom you may not have groomed a backup.

If you haven't done it—and done it lately—you should have every position in your company looked at, to tell you several things:

> Who these sensitive key employees are
>
> For each one, what the sudden loss or long absence of that person would cost, both in work interruption and, if it can be estimated, in dollars
>
> Who would—or could—step into the job in an emergency
>
> What the potential successor would have to learn, to do the job well

After you have identified the spots—the people and the requirements—you can and should start to prepare the potential successor with more work in the areas of his deficiency, and to test him and his training by on-the-job exposure. That can be done at vacation time, during an illness or other emergency, or possibly during a period of peak work load.

You may find that you have no one with the necessary background to build on, so that you will have to go outside; but this warning at least will give you more lead time.

While you are making such an inventory, you may learn things about the rest of your training and development program. Even in the positions that are not critically time-sensitive, your manpower and womanpower needs keep changing constantly, and you may find that your recruitment and training are not keeping in step. You could end up top-heavy in some areas of skill and too lean to meet competition in some other areas.

You might even find a few positions that have outlived their usefulness and are no longer needed at all. If you do, and act on it by moving the incumbent into more productive work, that alone would pay the cost of the inventory.

Nothing Succeeds Like Succession Planning

Q You have written about depth of management and the importance of having replacements ready to succeed those who retire or are suddenly removed from the picture. But is deliberate succession planning really practical? Doesn't something usually come along to upset all your plans and projections—you either lose the one you've been grooming or decide you need him somewhere else, or your needs change after you have done all the preparing? Isn't it cheaper and more feasible just to wait and see, and if you don't have the right person ready, go outside and hire him?

A If, as I believe, it is one of the two main responsibilities of the CEO to make sure that the right people are presently and prospectively in place to fill all the key jobs in the company, then it follows that there must be an organized, orderly program of succession planning.

The occasional unforeseen gap may be filled from the outside. But to fill all principal posts from the outside is to court serious internal problems: lowered morale generally, and above all greater difficulty in attracting and holding the most promising young people. They will gravitate toward the places where they can advance without limit: "Why should I stick around there if the good jobs are always going to go to somebody brought in from the outside?"

Succession planning can never be exact. Growth will create new positions demanding new capabilities; and even the apparently traditional jobs will change character as new technology and new patterns of business are introduced. And things do happen to the candidates who are being groomed: some will fail to measure up to early expectations, some may leave the company and some may be removed by death or health problems. But this attrition only adds to the importance of having at least the requisite number of people ready with the preparation they will need for each spot.

And what is that?

I always thought that the worst possible preparation was what the railroads traditionally gave their executives: If you were assigned as a young employee to the passenger department, in the passenger department you stayed until you retired, unless you were one of the three or four who emerged at the top to become chairman, president, or executive vice president. By that time you knew all about your half of the business, but your tunnel vision warped your view of everything else. Even after making allowance for all the other troubles railroads have faced—competition from trucks, pipelines, buses, and airlines— I always have charged part of their difficulties to this myopic personnel policy, which happily has disappeared now along with the passenger business.

Contrast this practice with that of A. P. Giannini, founder of Bank of America. He rarely promoted anyone in a straight-line vertical path: at all levels, progression was typically zigzag, from one specialized function to another. Even at the most senior levels he and his successor son Mario would uproot and zigzag people, pulling out the controller and putting him in charge of business development, transplanting the supervisor of domestic branches to head up international banking. There were often multiple motives in these diagonal moves—they forestalled empire building, which the Gianninis detested; sometimes they made better use of personal qualities in the new assignment—but always the benefits of cross-fertilization and exposure were clearly demonstrated.

What is needed for full preparation will vary from company to company, but a few ingredients are universal. The exact character of a machine-tool manufacturer's market will be different from that of a clothing manufacturer, but the interdependence of marketing, production, and finance are universal. The functions and people to be supervised will differ from one industry to another, but the importance of effective supervision is universal. The particular relation to government or to other segments of society will vary, but sensitivity to public concerns is an essential ingredient in general management.

How formally the executive development or management training programs are organized will depend upon the size of the company. But every company that expects to survive should study the ingredients of each position from middle to top management, examine the individuals who are likely to be candidates for each of those positions, and then map out programs that will expose each of them to anything that is now lacking in his or her equipment. For some it will involve job rotation or deviation in progression patterns. For some it will require special schooling, whether at one of the business schools or in one of the many specialized curricula now offered by colleges and universities. In some cases it will require only special counseling or guidance.

Not all of the training and exposure are on technical or management problems. Many companies have found that if their executives are going to be prepared for senior responsibility, they will have to know more about government, and have arranged government exchange programs. Others have gotten their people into community work—the United Way and the like—to broaden their contacts, increase their poise and self-confidence in public, and sharpen their leadership skills.

At least one company I know has enrolled some of its middle managers in liberal arts courses in nearby colleges to broaden their awareness of some cultural areas that had been left out of their early education. This employer has been highly pleased with the results—both on the job and off.

V

Leadership

Picking people, training them, and holding them are basic, but they still are only the foundation of the executive job. It is what those people *do* that pays off.

And what they do will depend on the kind of leadership they get—the sense of direction they feel and are given.

What Is Leadership?

Q I keep hearing and reading that "what we need is leadership." We need better leadership in government; we need better leadership in business; we need better leadership in our own company. But what is leadership, really? Can it be defined or identified, so that we will recognize it when we see it?

A To try to answer that within the confining limits of one chapter may seem foolish, if not impossible. But there is virtue in trying to reduce leadership down to its essentials.

In the most bare-bones definition, a leader is one whom others will follow willingly and voluntarily. That rules out tyrants, bullies, autocrats, and all those others who use coercive power to impose their wills on others.

But what are the qualities that cause people willingly and voluntarily to follow someone? They are few and they are plainly visible. Moreover—and this may seem more surprising—I believe that these qualities can be acquired; they can be learned, developed, and enhanced.

We hear of "born leaders"; and indeed some of the qualities do seem to appear at an early age and to remain as consistent earmarks and characteristics—not as things that appear suddenly, and certainly not as things that can be taught entirely in a course labeled Leadership 1a.

But I think that these qualities are the end product of all the learning experiences and influences that shape a character; and while most leaders have probably been shaped fortuitously, by the lucky accident of being exposed to mentors and experiences that put high premiums on the right qualities, other candidates for leadership who were able to identify the qualities and recognize their importance could have prepared themselves by their own deliberate efforts to strengthen these same qualities.

What are they?

People will follow the person who they feel

> Knows where he is going
>
> Knows how to get there
>
> Has courage and persistence—will not run away or back down from danger, opposition, or discouragement
>
> Can be believed
>
> Can be trusted not to sell their cause out for his personal advantage
>
> Makes the mission seem important, exciting, and possible to accomplish
>
> Makes their role in the mission seem important
>
> Makes them feel capable of performing their role

These same ingredients can be found in leaders of every kind of field—whether a country at war, a labor union, a football team, a radical political movement, or a private business. History-book accounts of earlier figures might seem glossed over; but within our own time we have had examples of leaders who clearly fitted these specifications. Winston Churchill, who may have been flawed in some other respects but never in his qualities of leadership, comes first to mind. Saul Aulinsky, the radical organizer of social reforms in Chicago, was totally different in personality and style, but he too had these essential ingredients.

A true leader has one quality that may not have to come into play very often, but that quickly identifies him when it does. If things have gone wrong in the company because people under an executive's command have made mistakes or performed badly, he might try to clear his skirts by criticizing those subordinates—to the board of directors, to investors, to the press. But the real leader does not hide behind others. He says one way or another: "I was responsible for what these people were doing, and I knew what they were doing" (or "I should have known what they were doing"), "so don't blame them—blame me."

He may have to do some disciplining, if people violated clear instructions, but he does not do it just to save his own skin. His troops will know it if he behaves that way, and will respect both his discipline and his subsequent leadership.

The popular—and superficial—image of a leader usually stresses his or her charisma—the physical attractiveness and charm that draw and hold attention. That might give the potential leader a head start while the more basic qualities had a chance to work; but the fact is that the more notable and durable leaders have not had it. Aulinsky did not; Churchill's was debatable.

A more relevant ingredient, which I did not list only because it is not a distinguishing one, is a skill that is needed for success in almost every setting: articulateness, the ability to communicate. Without that, the other attributes do not have a chance to show.

Where the potential leader most often falls short—and where the real leader most distinguishes himself from the driver—is in the last two qualities listed above: those that give the followers faith in themselves.

The world is full of take-charge types who do take charge and who achieve tremendous results without having these last two qualities. They have all the other attributes I have named, but not these two; so they get results. As someone once said, "The world stands aside for the man who knows where is is going."

In many of the world's work situations that alone is enough to get the work done.

But it is not leadership. It might then be asked, "So what? Who needs more than getting the work done?" There are times in every country, every company, and every organization when much more is needed than just getting the day's work done—although even the day's work soon ceases to be done as well, if that extra factor is missing.

That extra factor is morale. I have written elsewhere in this book about morale and its ingredients. It is closely allied to the concept of leadership, and particularly to those last two qualities.

Even in ordinary circumstances, good morale can have a tonic effect, and a measurable effect, on productivity. But when survival is threatened—in a company or a country—morale is more than a tonic; it is a lifesaver.

And leadership can make that crucial difference in morale.

Lundborg's Laws

Q I once read in an article you had written a list of some eight or ten points you called "Lundborg's Laws." They struck me as a good checklist for executives. Could you reprint this?

A While the whole article, spelling out each of the so-called "Laws," would fill too many pages, here is a boiled-down version:

Law #1 *MULTIPLY YOURSELF.*
Don't try to do it all yourself.

Law #2 *PICK WINNERS.*
Good people are tough to get, tough to manage, and tough to hang on to—but good people cost less because of their greater output.

Law #3 *DON'T SETTLE FOR SECOND BEST.*
The greatest enemy is mediocrity—and the only alternative is excellence.

Law #4 *LET THEM RUN.*
If you have picked winners, you won't cash in on them unless you let them run.

Law #5 *DON'T ALIBI.*
When things go wrong, don't make excuses, and don't pass the buck—upward, downward, or laterally.

Law #6 *BE A CLOCK WATCHER.*
Be a good manager of time.

Law #7 *DON'T BE A DEAF MUTE.*
Communicate—and do it with your ears as well as your eyes.

Law #8 *KEEP YOUR MOTOR TUNED AND YOUR OIL CHANGED.*
Stay healthy.

Executive or Manager?

Q You sometimes use the word "manager" and sometimes "executive." Are they the same?

A I hope I have not used them synonymously because they are not the same. Some people are both; but there are managers who are not executives, and executives who are not managers—at least as I am using the words. Peter Drucker has made the distinction, in several of his books; and I am accepting his definitions because they stress functions that I think are vital to an understanding of the executives's role. And that is what this book is all about.

Drucker calls "executives" those who are expected by virtue of their position or knowledge to make decisions in the normal course of their work that have significant impact on the performance and results of the whole enterprise. Such people, he points out, may be found at all levels of the company, and they may do the same kind of work as the president of the company, that is, plan, organize, integrate, motivate, and measure. Their scope may be limited; but within that scope, they are executives.

As he also points out, there are many managers who are not executives. As supervisors, they manage the work of others, often large numbers of others; but they are not responsible for, and do not have authority over, the direction, content, or quality of the work. And there are executives who are not managers, in the sense that they do not have any group of workers to supervise, but who make decisions that contribute significantly to the results of the company.

It is because decision making is so central a part of the executive's role that I have so often tried to highlight elements in a company that tend to help or to hinder decisiveness. Yet decisions and decisiveness are in themselves only a means toward a larger end: effectiveness. The successful executive is one who is effective in advancing whatever is his contribution to the capacity of his organization to perform and obtain results.

What I have said from time to time about managing and supervising the work of others to get the best performance and results still applies whether or not the manager is also an executive. Both manager and executive should seek to be effective, but each has a different goal for his effectiveness.

There are, of course, many executives who are also managers. They are responsible for getting maximum performance and results from the work of others, so they are managers. But they have responsibility and authority to make decisions that might improve the capacity and ability to perform, so they also are executives.

In any case, "executive" is not just a high-falutin name for "manager." They are two honorable functions, but different.

Survival of
Women-Owned Businesses

Q We hear and read a lot about women moving into more senior executive positions in corporations. But even when women own and operate their own businesses, some of them seem to have difficulty in being successful managers and executives. Why is that?

A This reply should not be addressed to women, although they are welcome to read it. It is addressed to men, with the warning "These things can happen to you too." If anything in it appears chauvinistic, it is accidental; because no comparison of men and women is intended at all.

We have the happy circumstance that separate studies have been made recently of businesses owned by women. And while the published results of these studies purport to deal with the special problems that women encounter when they run their own businesses, what they really do is highlight the universal problems of the small-business operator, male or female.

Many of these problems get exaggerated for women simply because women have not historically been given exposure to the kinds of experience that would prepare them for what they have to do as owner-operators. (Even that lack of preparation is not the exclusive property of women: many men have been plunged into owner-manager or corporate-manager positions without adequate preparation for the special requirements of the manager.)

Bank of America has probably made more loans to small business enterprises than any other bank in the world. Out of this experience its loan officers have acquired unusual insight in what makes small businesses succeed or fail.

There are some common denominators that run through all types of businesses: when one of them fails, or runs into serious near-failure difficulties, it rarely is because of any shortcoming in the techniques or special know-how of that business. If it is a repair garage, no one is complaining that the cars are not properly repaired. If it is a furniture-refinishing establishment, there is no problem about the workmanship there either. What gets them into difficulty is their failure to *manage*. That in turn usually resolves itself down into one or both of two problems: problems with money, and problems with people.

One of the most universal mistakes people make in starting new businesses is their failure to forecast their money needs and to make sure they have adequate capital to meet them, and a universal problem among small businesses is the managing of people. The founder of the new small business may have great skill in doing things himself. But when he starts to multiply himself by hiring others to work for him, he has entered a completely new world. Motivating these new employees to get the most and best work from them; keeping them all working in harmony with each other; making sure that treatment of customers does not drive business out the back door as fast as advertising and sales effort can bring customers in the front door; making sure that employees understand the importance of everything they are doing in keeping customers satisfied and in keeping costs down—all these things, and many more like them, are new and different from what the new entrepreneur used to do when he worked for someone else.

The women-owned businesses had the same pattern of problems—although the women involved tend to describe them as if only women had them. Their failure to do proper financial planning they explain by saying that fear of accounting and math often discourages women from diagnosing the condition of their companies and from planning their direction. They did not know what break-even or cash flow was; nor did they know better than to seek a bank loan without a company financial statement to support it. Men who have been through the same syndrome could simply say, "Welcome to the club."

The people-management area is only slightly different. Companies get into trouble, whether they are run by men or women, if the boss does not manage the people under him to get the best performance from them. Truth to tell, many women have had difficulty in establishing that they *are* the boss, in a world that has been dominated by male bosses. But more have had difficulty because they were *afraid* they would not be respected than because their subordinates refused to follow them. And again, men who have not been accustomed to the command role and are timid about it have the same problem.

The key in both cases is the same, and it is not just to overcompensate by being "bossy." For a woman it is, first, to demonstrate that she knows her business: there are men who refuse to follow the orders of a woman simply because they think she doesn't know what she is talking about (some new, raw male bosses have the same trouble). After that, if they still don't follow orders, she will have to state calmly but firmly that she is giving the instructions, that she expects them to be followed, and that anyone who chooses not to follow them will not be working there any more.

And she must mean it. Firing an employee is not easy for any boss, man or woman. But fairness to the productive, cooperative employee occasionally requires removing those who are not.

There are women who are miscast as managers, whether as owners or as employed executives. Some of them are going to fail. But rarely if at all will it be because they are women.

Technician or Manager?

Q What can a middle manager do to raise his chances of advancing to a high position (e.g., plant manager) when upper management puts excessive value on administrative ability, overlooking the need for technical competence? Or am I wasting my time even thinking about it?

A You are not wasting your time if you *really* think about it, and then do something about it.

The first question for you to think out is whether your upper management people are not right in putting high value on administrative and executive ability when they are considering candidates for higher managerial jobs. They know that the job of the manager is to manage—not just to do things himself, but to get things done. That means getting things done through other people.

Your top people may appreciate technical competence more than you realize; but they don't confuse it with managerial competence, which is a different animal. The same person may happen to have both, and certainly the technician can learn to improve his managerial skills if he has a genuine interest in doing so. If he hasn't, it could be a disservice to him as well as to the company to promote him to a managerial position *only* as a reward for his technical contributions. A lot of what we ascribe to the Peter Principle results from that kind of rewarding.

So the next question you should ask yourself is whether you ever have shown managerial ability, and if not, whether you are willing to do what is necessary to acquire it. Managing is a learned skill; some have more natural aptitude and learn more easily than others, but everyone can improve his skills by effort and application.

While you are learning, you will need to factor in another ingredient that is one of the key differences between a technician and a manager: perspective. The very nature of the technician's job usually demands that he focus on one problem at a time, and even one small piece of the problem—he is dealing with one piece of the jigsaw puzzle. The manager's job requires him to be constantly aware of all the pieces of the puzzle—to see that they all fit together at the right time and in the right sequence. Both of these are valuable and essential functions in a company's operation; they just involve a different perspective.

Again there is nothing about the managerial perspective that cannot be learned. But you first need to ask yourself if your years as a technical expert have not developed such a habit of using a peep-sight focus on technical details that you will have a difficult time, at first, retraining your peripheral vision to see things whole.

And ask yourself if you really want to make the change. Many people who are called managers, and should be spending 90% of their time on management work, just won't let go of the technical work. They feel more comfortable doing the familiar technical job; and of course hands-on work is often more fun. So they make all kinds of excuses—pressure of deadlines, shortage of experienced personnel—for not delegating the technical work as completely as they should, but immersing themselves in it at the expense of their real responsibility, managing.

It is a universal enough tendency that Louis A. Allen, consultant and lecturer on management development, has coined what he calls "The Principle of Technical Priority," which he says explains why managers often find themselves buried under work other people should be doing. His principle holds that "when called upon to perform both management work and technical work during the same period, managers tend to give priority to technical work."

Perhaps your top management people have observed you yielding to that temptation.

In any case, if you want to move out of the technician's into the manager's role, you must reorient, regroove, and retrain yourself. You can start right where you are, becasue I gather that you are manager of a group of technicians. Let your senior management people see you *managing* your group—developing *their* skills, getting the most and best work out of *them*—instead of demonstrating your own "technical competence."

But be sure that a manager's role is what you want.

Paying the Specialist

Q I have a man in my company who is a high-quality and high-quantity producer—but strictly a solo performer. He is not interested in managing a large department, and I'm not sure he would do it well; but he makes a lot of money for us where he is, because he attracts business and is imaginative in how to solve customers' problems. Our problem is how to compensate him. If we paid him what he thinks (and I think) he is worth, he would be making more than the head of the department he is in. Our personnel people tell me we can't do that—that it would upset our whole salary administration. But he really belongs in that department for other operating reasons; and his work does not lend itself to paying him on commission, which might simplify our problem. Can you suggest any other answer?

A My first answer is to tell your personnel department that it should not get so locked into formulas and procedures that it can't deal with problems. Salary administration is intended to help company operations—not vice versa.

100

Yours is not a unique problem, and it may become more common in today's world. We have always had a few situations described as "They took a good teacher and made a poor principal of her" or "They ruined a good salesman to make a lousy salesmanager." Those situations reflected a universal tendency (not always expressed but implicit in many salary structures) to equate the importance of a person's job with the number of people under the person's command. That thinking contributed to the empire-building ambitions of many a bureaucrat, both in government and in business.

It also has been the root cause of many cases that have been wrongly labeled as examples of the Peter Principle: people being promoted to the level of their incompetence. In many of these cases it is not level of incompetence—it is "level of least interest" or "least challenge."

But many developments of recent years have brought the traditional thinking even more into question. The explosion of technology and of the "knowledge industries" has spawned a new breed of specialists who have their own place—and their own value—in the business picture. The field of executive search has made its contribution to this development, but whether executive search stimulated executive mobility, or whether mobility paved the way for the headhunters, is immaterial here. The fact is that specialists, of the kind you mention, are now highly mobile.

These are the facts that you must deal with in working out your problem.

I am a little surprised that it is your personnel department that is balking: modern personnel managers usually recognize what has to be done. More typically the problem is with the immediate supervisor—the head of the department or unit to whom the specialist reports. His pride gets tweaked if anyone in his department is paid more than he is. Here is where you will have to use your managerial skill.

First of course you, with the collaboration of your personnel manager, must come to some reasonable measure of the specialist's value. (And remember that if you don't do that, some headhunter may do it for you.)

Then—whether the department head has objected or not—you should be sure that he understands several things about this situation: First, this specialist is not just another employee. He provides (in the case of most specialists, at least) a market-value service that you might have chosen to retain on the outside, at probably greater cost, but that you prefer to have in-house. Second, the department head has many things going for him that the specialist does not: the specialist is not a member of the management team, and does not have the promotional opportunities open to him that the department head does.

This is a real-life situation, and it may not be the last one you will have to face in your company. Each one is a special case, and the treatment has to be custom-tailored; but you will have to live with the hierarchical problem while dealing with the real problem of value.

The Helping Relationship

Q I often hear it said that a good executive, or a good supervisor at any level, is a helper to those under his direction. But doesn't that really weaken them, by acting as a crutch and making them more dependent?

A Not if the "help" is of the right kind. I have always warned against "upstream delegation," sometimes known as letting your subordinates put the monkey on your back by subtly getting you to do part of their jobs for them. That *is* weakening.

But it is not weakening to be sure that the subordinate knows how to do the job. If the job is a manual or a mechanical operation, there is nothing wrong with going through a demonstration of the correct method; you obviously wouldn't consider going on from there to complete the employee's entire day's work.

The more critical area is the one in which the subordinate must make decisions, write statements, or otherwise exercise individual judgments. If you let yourself make those decisions or write that copy (even by editing the subordinate's draft), you may take on the care and feeding of the subordinate's monkey.

What you can do is to be sure that he has asked himself all the right questions before arriving at his own decisions. A supervisor *should* be a teacher; but what you must teach your subordinate to do is to stand on his own feet.

The supervisor who is a good teacher does not even insist on his own method as being the only right one. What he is trying to give his pupil is confidence in the ability to get the job done well. Usually that works best by teaching the traditional method first and letting the pupil add any variations later. But in any case the teacher only points the way, and makes the pupil do the work—at any level, from assembly line to executive suite.

N.B. Beware of the supervisor who is Dr. Jekyll to you and Mr. Hyde to the people under him. He will cause trouble for you by creating turmoil and ill will in his unit. That kind of person has a problem and may be helped by counseling; but if not, he is a poor risk in an organization.

Selling—or Report Writing?

Q Our company operates a steel-products distribution network with yards and offices throughout the country. Our problem stems from natural reluctance of busy administrators and salespeople to generate the reports and studies needed to keep management informed. How can we keep managers and salespeople of the will-do, can-do type from neglecting the routine reporting needed to keep planning for growth and customer service at its best?

A Your problem is not unique. It seems to exist wherever there are salespeople and reports. Almost by definition, good salespeople are people who don't like to write reports—they would rather be out selling. Yet management needs reports.

The first question is, How many and what kind? Since the birth of the computer and its godchildren, management information systems, there has been constant danger of our becoming report-happy. Equally a booby trap is the assumption that every data stream into the computer must be uniform and everybody on that stream must report in identically the same fashion. That one needs to be broken open a bit: your data-systems people should recognize differences.

Before we talk about specific solutions to your problem, let me tell you about a company that went to the opposite extreme away from requiring reports: A highly successful food-products company, now swallowed up in a huge conglomerate, would not even tell the top sales manager what was happening to the company's earnings or involve him in budget making. The CEO simply told him, "Never mind bothering yourself with a lot of accounting numbers—you just go out and sell boxes." He did, and the company prospered.

Obviously that kind of seat-of-the-pants approach won't entirely fit into today's finance- and investment-oriented management—but the spririt of it can be salvaged. Here are a few things you can do:

While the sales *department* may have to comply with the standard reporting requirements, the sales*people* don't all have to be involved. Try to limit the reports made by salespeople only to information directly involved in their work, which is calling on customers and prospects to make sales. Let someone else in the department put together the other reports—budgets, projections, etc. And make even the required reports as easy as possible for the salespeople to make. Simplify the reporting forms so that the information you need can be easily filled in. Some companies have used a variety of oral reporting routines to good advantage: as one sales manager says, "Salesmen hate to write reports, but I never saw one who didn't like to talk." He has the salesmen phone their reports to one of his assistants, who is skilled enough that she not only records what they volunteer but draws additional information out of them by questioning.

Some companies use their regular sales meetings as the vehicle for extracting oral reports. Particularly for the nonsales kind of data that you simply have to have to run your department—budget projections, for example. A typical salesperson could agonize over one of those for hours or days at his desk; but when it is being talked out with his peers around a table, he can piece together most of it before he leaves the meeting. He may want to correct a figure or two, but the "report writing" will already have been done by the secretary of the meeting.

Incidentally, if you do decide to have reports phoned in or orally developed in a meeting, then typed up by a secretary or administrative assistant, it is prudent to have the salesperson initial a copy.

Preparation of the studies you mention—which I assume are such things as market projections—is more of a staff than a line job, and is an ideal exposure for a young staff person with good potential. Sales managers are typically no more enthusiastic about writing up such studies than they—or their sales troops—are about any other kinds of reports; but they are likely to respond quite readily to oral probing by the staff person.

A few companies have used an incentive element to drag reports out of reluctant salespeople. Where continuing customer cultivation is almost as important as immediate sales in the long-range marketing plans, it is important to know not only that calls have been made, but what kinds of calls, on what kinds of companies, with what kinds of results. In these cases, a small but significant increment of bonus points is figured into the calculation of commissions or bonuses for the completion—and reporting—of the expected number of calls. There are some built-in hazards in such a system (such as weaker salesmen rushing around at month-end to make perfunctory calls just to qualify), but in special situations it is worth considering.

One report that salespeople seldom are backward about writing is the expense account. As a last resort you can use it as a discipline by requiring that the specified reports be submitted with the expense account. But first try the other ways of making it easier—and if possible, more interesting—for them to give you the reports you need.

You still want to keep these can-do people spending most of their energy on the things they do best.

Expense-Account Entertaining

Q Even before Jimmy Carter started preaching about the evils of the three-martini lunch, I had begun to question whether we were getting our money's worth out of all the expense-account entertaining being done by our salesmen and some of our other people—our service representatives and even our more senior executives.

What do you think: does entertaining a customer or a prospect really pay off in new business? And if so, how do I gauge how much, and what kinds, should be approved?

A So much political guff and other nonsense have been turned loose by that three-martini remark that it has clouded over the business basics of the issue. Since I am not writing tax advice or political opinion, I won't debate here whether entertainment expense should be deductible for tax purposes. You should not let that debate distort your business judgment about other aspects that are more important than the tax consequences.

The first thing to get straight and clear is that in most industries, entertainment does not buy much business—and what it does buy doesn't stay bought very long. That is not why the prudent manager encourages customer entertainment. A wise sales manager once observed that "if a pint will get an order, a quart will take it away."

The real reason why we entertain customers—and prospects— is to get to know them and their needs. The best selling is always aimed at studying the customer's needs and trying to fill them. The off-premises visit, away from telephones and other interruptions, is often the best setting in which to pursue that—often but not always. Every case is different; and your representative must be perceptive enough to know which ones are which.

A related reason for entertaining is to establish your sales representative as more than "just a salesman" (whatever that is— an unfair but common put-down of a respected calling); it should help him to gain acceptance as a friend dealing with his customer on an equal footing and as one who can be trusted and respected when he recommends products to solve special problems. (Incidentally, if your representative is not one who can be expected to gain trust and respect, you should not allow him to go near a customer, with or without an expense account.)

The sales representative is not the only one in your company who might need to buy someone's lunch and should not be expected to pay for it out of his own pocket. If you have a public relations department that deals with the press and the electronic media, or community relations people who deal with school, church, or civic leaders, or general executives who must meet with their counterparts on industry matters—any of these will need, once in a while, to invite someone to lunch where problems can be discussed away from the pressure of a formal meeting.

But again the same rules of the game apply: your man (or woman—because this is a coeducational process) is not trying to "buy" anyone's vote or cooperation. He or she is trying the same thing the sales rep is doing: to build understanding, trust, and confidence.

That says something about how the entertaining should be done. A lavish spread of food and drink, reminiscent of Diamond Jim Brady in the era of the big spenders, is not the atmosphere that inspires trust and confidence. On the contrary, the guest is going to suspect he is being conned into something and will be more than ever on his guard.

Good taste is hard to define, but a safe rule for your people to remember is that the entertaining is not intended to make a dazzling impression on anyone, (the expense account is not designed to enable either your representative or his guest to live high on the hog) and that the place selected should be a good restaurant, hotel, or club that might be assumed to be within the means and normal habits of either host or guest—at the upper edge of the range, perhaps, but not so far beyond as to be "putting on airs."

In these terms, expense-account entertaining is another business tool, not a privilege of rank. Like any other business tool— telephone, travel, postage, added personnel, enlarged quarters—it can be abused, or it can be used to produce results. Anyone who cannot be trusted to use and not abuse any of these tools is probably not a good bet to entrust with any of the other responsibilities of his job!

But you have a responsibility here too. First of all, you owe it to your associates, as well as to yourself, to make sure that they understand this point of view. And then, as part of your total job of monitoring their performance, you should satisfy your-

self that they are putting it into practice: not by your flyspecking every item of expense, but by seeing whether they are getting results.

P.S. No matter who pays for them—expense account or not—
nobody who drinks three martinis for lunch is going to survive
in business competition.

Know-It-All—or Helper?

Q I work for a family business in which I'm the youngest partner.

How does one go about making improvements which are needed but which are really not in my area? I hate to have the older partners think I am a "know it all."

Although I hate to make waves, I cannot stand to see money wasted.

A Your position is not materially different from that of any other junior executive, except in one important detail: you *are* a partner. So you are entitled to express your views, even outside your area. I remind you of that, not with the thought that you should bumptiously "demand" to be heard, but so that you can be relaxed in your feeling that you are not out of order. You are pursuing your responsibility as a partner—just as an officer of a corporation would be, in the same circumstances.

There is nothing wrong with making waves. In fact, most of the people who have moved up very far in any company have been the ones who did occasionally stir up the waters. But they also were usually the ones who had answers to suggest for any problems they uncovered. That should be part of your approach.

I have to assume, with no more facts than you have given me, that your family partners have at least one interest in common, and that is to make the company as profitable as possible. Each of your partners may have a different idea of how that can be done. What you should try first is to find ways in which your proposed improvements would benefit some activity or project that each of the other partners considers important. In that way you might be able to gain their support not as a "know it all" but as one whose ideas appeal to their own self-interest. That is the basis of most good selling, including the selling of ideas.

VI

The Other End of the Line—Retirement and Terminations

Hiring the right people, training them, and preparing them for advancement through the company are only one side of the coin. The other side involves what happens to those people as they reach retirement age.

The two sides of that coin—and the way each side affects the other—together present management with one of its knottier problems. Not all parts of that problem leave neat, tidy solutions; and some of the solutions have created new problems of their own.

Because this matter is so fluid, and because so much of it is affected by forces outside management's immediate control, it is another real test of the art of being an executive.

Stepping Down

Q I started my business from scratch thirty years ago and still own enough stock to have control. I'm sixty-eight but the company and I are both healthy, making money every year, and I don't see any reason to retire. All these hints I get—"Turn the reins over to someone younger"—sound smart, but they're poppycock. None of the younger ones could run the business the way I do. Why should I pay any attention? What's the right age for a man to step down?

A There is no right age, and no exact right time. But there are several wrong times, based not on age so much as on your own mental attitude.

If you're sure nobody else can run the business, so that you're going to keep looking over your successor's shoulder, constantly jostling his (or her) elbow telling him what to do—forget it. He will prove you're correct; he won't be able to run the business. But it will be your fault, not his.

Even worse, don't be like one founder-operator I watched. He brought in one man after another from the outside. Like many founders, he had never groomed a successor—partially because deep down he was sure he was going to live forever, and partially because, like you, he knew that no one else could run the business as well as he did. So he brought each of these people in one by one, and chewed them up and spit them out like so many grape seeds. It was quite plain that he was simply salving his own ego, and proving to his critics that he was better than any of these young whippersnappers. He never gave any of them the authority to do the job, and he made it a no-win game. The better ones enraged him by the hint that somebody else could run the company, and the weak ones just confirmed his prejudice.

Now on the more affirmative side, let's look at some of the reasons why there must eventually be succession, reasons why you should want to be in full command of planning and implementing it, and some of the factors influencing the timing.

One of the major reasons for any retirement program is not to get rid of the older incumbents, but to make room for the younger people to move up. If the word gets around that you won't give up until they carry you out, the more ambitious (and more promising) of your subordinates will hunt for greener pastures. Equally bad, it will get harder and harder to attract the best young blood to the company, so it will lose some vigor before you know it. You'll be all the more convinced that none of the young have got your spark.

So you do not want to wait until the slow-down hits your company. Start your move while your momentum is at a peak.

Among the factors by which managers are judged (and by which the investment fraternity judges a company) is the depth of management and the preparation for succession. Those judgments may not seem important to you now, but you have to pick between

1. The momentary ego massage of feeling that you are so smart and capable that no one can take your place
2. The most lasting satisfaction of building something so strong that it will survive you, and will grow, expand, and improve on the base you've built

Once you make the basic choice, the time frame comes into focus: if you actually do have someone in-house who would make a completely suitable successor, then you can start things into motion immediately. But if you don't, then what you start into motion is the search (from inside or outside), and then the necessary exposure and preparation. All this you should want to do while you're sure that you'll be around long enough to see it through. You know more than anybody about the job, and that wisdom needs to be passed along while you're at your best.

The transition time is delicate, of course, very much like the time when one relay runner passes the baton to his teammate. One founder-CEO has just reversed the habits of a lifetime: he still offers information and advice aplenty but never "follows up." That's how he makes it clear that he's not giving orders.

Then: The real payoff will come when you can take honest pride in your new CEO's unique style. On the day you know he made a decision better than you'd have made it, you will have truly earned the right to consider yourself a fine chief executive.

The Fraud of Flexible-Age Retirement

Q Doesn't the recent legislation to outlaw compulsory retirement correct a lot of injustices, and in the process solve some tough problems for management?

A No.

In the emotional frenzy to push through laws to abolish mandatory retirement at age sixty-five, our state and federal governments have unthinkingly traded supposed inhumanity in one form for inhumanity in another. It is a bad trade. The consequences will plague this country as long as the laws in their present form remain on the books.

To get the problem into perspective, let me "stipulate," as the lawyers would say: there is no such thing as a completely good retirement system that will fit all kinds of companies. A few have been able to tailor some near-ideal plans that fit their unusual circumstances; but for the majority of companies, the best that can be said is that uniform compulsory retirement at some fixed age was the least of the evils. There was nothing sacred about age sixty-five, which had dubious origins as the arbitrary cut-off point; but it served to minimize the problems that would have been (and will now be) created by anything more than a year or two above that age.

The virtue of compulsory retirement was that everyone who reached that point could walk out with his head held high and say to himself, "I'm still in good shape, and if it weren't for that damned retirement program I could go on working for a long time yet." But the moment an employer is able to pick and choose on the basis of health and performance, it is saying in effect to one employee, "You, Smith—you're a young vigorous 65; you can stay on. But you, Jones—you're all burned out and you're not cutting the mustard. You're out." That is great for Smith's morale, but it utterly destroys Jones.

The problems of the employer in trying to cope with this new tangle of administrative and regulatory burdens are horrendous. At best, the procedures to justify each separation will impose another layer of "compliance" and paperwork burdens on top of ERISA, OSHA, EEOC, wage and price guidelines, and all the rest. At worst, the lawsuits that may grow out of these separations could make this another of the "Lawyers' Relief Acts."

But the administrative side of the problem fades in comparison to the human problems. Running all through this issue are one or both of two motives: to support the dignity and self-respect of the individual employee, and to support the freedom of the employer to manage. These two objectives are always potentially in conflict; but in this case they need not be, unless they are swept under the rug on the assumption that all the problems were solved by the passage of the recent legislation.

The ironic twist to this entire scenario is that the push to change the retirement practices, presumably to correct an inequity, came from the same place where the worst part of the problem had been created in the first place: the federal government. But the government's prescription was not designed to treat the ailments it had generated, but to divert attention away from those to other symptoms.

While there has been scattered comment for many years about the "great waste of human talent" that resulted from retiring people "right at the peak of their powers," nothing really happened. There was no real movement or organized campaign to outlaw that retirement until it became apparent that the Social Security fund was in serious trouble. Then the legislation was rushed through with a minimum of study, hearings, or debate on the side effects.

A few years ago I had a conversation with the then head of a major oil company that had had a long-standing policy of retiring its upper-echelon executives—not everyone in the company, but something like the top forty—at age sixty. I had just previously been involved in defending the compulsory-retirement-at-sixty-five pattern; and I said to my friend, "If it is true, as I have been hearing, that it is wasteful and unfair to retire people at sixty-five, it must be doubly so to retire them as you do, at age sixty." His reply was "Not so. If anyone is good enough to be one of our top forty people, he will still be marketable at age sixty—he can get into a new career that might not have any age limit at all. The proof of the pudding," he added, "is that practically all of our people who have retired under that rule have done just that."

Now I am quite aware that people at upper executive levels have quite a different market for their talents than have those in lower echelons of employment (although the comparison is not entirely one-sided). But the real point is that many employed persons at all levels have other talents and skills than those at which they are now employed; and while they might not be able to earn as much if they switched to another job or activity, there is something demeaning in the assumption that there is a "waste of human talent" if they do not continue in their present corporate employment—that that is the only way to "utilize their powers to the fullest." There is a hint of involuntary servitude in that concept.

Financial Security
for Older Workers

Q What about financial security for older workers? Doesn't the raising or removal of the age of mandatory retirement ease that problem?

A Financial security is quite another matter. No matter when a worker finally retires—no matter at what age—he is headed for a sad end unless some sound financial provision has been made for him, either by his own efforts or by his employer. No system of fixed-income pensions can be adequate in the face of inflation; and few private employers could afford the risk of setting up variable ("indexed") pensions, with built-in hedges against inflation.

It is bitterly ironic that the very group—the officials of government, whose continued deficit financing and spending have done the most to fuel the inflation that is robbing others of their savings and their future security—have nicely protected themselves by voting themselves escalating pensions.

123

Not only are the basic pensions of federal employees more generous than those of private-salaried employees in comparable positions, but they are subject to cost-of-living adjustment, so that in this era of inflation they are adjusted upward twice a year for inflation. Most private employers do make some adjustment periodically, but few if any could afford to do what the federal government and some state governments have done.

A government employee can retire at age fifty-five with full retirement benefits. Assuming that he retires at that age with a pension of $20,000 a year and that he lives twenty-two more years; if inflation continues at a $6\frac{1}{2}\%$ annual rate, his pension in twenty-two years will be about $80,000 a year. If a private employee retires with a $20,000 pension, he could still be getting only $20,000 twenty-two years later.

Many of the state governments have installed similar cost-of-living adjustments in their pensions, but none more generously than was done in California—for the top officials only. The other state employees' pensions are adjusted annually by the same percentage as the consumer price index. But the so-called "constitutional officers"—the elected statewide officials—have a formula that builds *three* cost-of-living escalators into their pension: their basic pension is based, not on their own final salary, but on that of the current incumbent in that office (which has kept moving upward and will probably continue to do so); then there is the "catch-up," an arbitrary adjustment for inflation since 1954; and finally there is the annual adjustment tied to the price index.

The result is that if inflation continues at even a 6% annual rate and if the present incumbents survive even twenty-years of retirement, their pensions at that point will be an estimated three times the *active salaries* of the future incumbents, and as much as six times as much as their own final salaries.

It has amazed me that no one has started a drive to expel from public office everyone who has participated in this flagrant self-dealing on pensions. In the parlance of the streets, they have "cut themselves a nice piece of cake"—and at the expense of people who cannot provide the same thing for themselves. And these anti-inflation cushions are in themselves a secondary contributor to inflation, as all built-in escalations are.

One reason why there was not more outcry at the time this self-serving legislation was being enacted was that it was done so quietly. And it was more than a coincidence that just as the unabated upsurge of inflation was making the future most frightening, and as it was becoming more and more apparent that Social Security was entirely failing of its declared mission (if, indeed, not being totally bankrupt), the Congressional move to outlaw mandatory retirement should be mounted, thereby diverting attention at least momentarily away from what was happening on these other fronts.

Meanwhile the new retirement rules have other side effects and social consequences that are equally bad; and each of these in turn will give rise to others, so that the "ripple effect" is hard to calculate. They do not all involve the aged.

To put one of these into perspective, it must be understood that pensions have always had a multiple purpose: in addition to providing, hopefully, financial security for workers in their old age, they were intended to make room for young people—to provide opportunity for upward mobility and growth. Rarely did an employer think only, if at all, about getting rid of the old; in fact, employers were as aware as any social scientist of the assets they were losing in the retirement of capable people. But they knew that they could never hold—or motivate—the most promising young people if the opportunity for advancement was shut off by keeping aging employees indefinitely on the payroll.

Case histories abound of companies that died because they went to seed—and they went to seed because they brought in no new blood as their original executives and employees began to age. They didn't bring in new blood because they couldn't: talented young people would not go to work for a company where their progress would be blocked by older people who were never going to retire.

An example is a California printing and stationery firm that proudly boasted that it had no pension plan. It had none because, it said, it needed none: no one ever had to retire as long as he could come to work. Some employees did indeed reach the point where they could not come to work, and there was no financial provision for them at all unless they had managed to save and invest; others went on and on until there were vice presidents in their seventies or older. The company for a long time dominated its field; but little by little it lost ground to its competitors with younger, more aggressive personnel. Finally the owners were compelled to sell in order to salvage even a portion of their investment. The acquiring company had a long-standing policy of retiring at sixty-five; and it was not prepared to breach that policy. So the over-age employees were promptly let out just at a point in their lives when they could least afford or cope with their termination.

The full impact of this aspect of the new retirement rules has not yet been felt; but it will be, in many and subtle ways.

Side Effects of Flexible-Age Retirement on Younger Workers

Q You have talked about the effects of the flexible-age retirement legislation on older workers; but are there other side effects, on younger workers and job seekers, for example?

A Indeed there are. At the other end of the scale, there will always be some people out of work at ages below the traditional retirement age level. And just as the minimum-wage law has operated to freeze the least competent workers out of employment (thereby damaging the very people the law was nominally designed to protect), so the new restrictions on mandatory retirement will make employers more reluctant than ever to hire workers who are in or above their middle age. Companies will already have enough problems in dealing with their marginal cases—employees who are no longer performing well and who also happen to be in their middle to upper sixties—without deliberately taking on new employees who might soon become the same kind of problem.

Corollary to this is a new trend that is already beginning to surface: the culling out at a much earlier age of people who are judged to be "deadwood"—those no longer performing up to expectations, and even some who are still competent but showing signs of slowing down so that soon they would present a performance problem. Companies that in the past would have "carried" such employees out to retirement at sixty-five now will be more inclined to terminate them early, before any age discrimination can be made.

The pressure to improve productivity in order to remain competitive simply reinforces this trend toward earlier screening out.

This earlier screening, in turn, adds additional pressure on employers to develop objective standards of competence and performance by which employees, young or old, can be judged. As Peter Drucker has pointed out, this is especially difficult, but also especially important, in the so-called "knowledge industries," which are employing a larger and larger part of the labor force. In any industry, as he further projects, if there are no criteria for competence for younger people and no regular review of their performance against the standards, any claim of incompetence against an older person is likely to be overturned as age discrimination.

At whatever age people are finally obliged to retire, the abruptness of their separation is often the most traumatic part of the experience—both financially and emotionally. The companies that have been able to devise plans for gradual phasing out over a period of a few years have done a more humane job for their employees—and in many cases a more profitable one for the company. Where the retiree was an executive with heavy, complex responsibilities, the transition has been smooth; the preparation of the successor was more thorough, and there was less time lost while the successor came up to speed.

Meanwhile the retiree was given more time to prepare himself for his new status: either to look for new employment, to set up a business of his own, to adjust his family living pattern (often one of the most acute problems because the fully employed person has neither time nor energy to address himself adequately to all the new problems he and his family will face).

There is not room within the scope of this chapter to deal adequately with all the adjustment problems and with some of the things that can be done to cope with them; but let me say only that the old saw of the man who told his wife, when he was about to retire, that she must be prepared to have half as much money and twice as much husband is no joke. Nor is the other one, "I married him for better or for worse, but not for lunch." These are all individual problems, to be solved by each retiree in his or her own way; but they *are* problems. And while there is no way to be sure the solutions will work until they are tried, the odds are vastly better if there is time to think about and to weigh alternatives before the day suddenly arrives.

Such a transition period, such a "phasing-out-phasing-in," would help to soften one other traumatic blow, especially for the retiring executive: One day he has a purpose in life, a place in which to operate, an office to handle correspondence, phone calls, visitors, etc. The next day he has none of it. He is a man without a country. If he belongs to a club, he can go there—but then what? He can drink, perhaps play a little bridge or dominoes. But they do not fill the gap. They only add to his deterioration.

Even with a transition period, such adjustments are not easy to make; but they are no easier at a higher age—and they can be shattering when the change is abrupt.

Overhanging all this, for both the employer and the employee, is the difficulty of planning for the future. Life is never totally predictable for anyone, but a new dimension of unpredictability has been added. For the well-managed company, staff planning is a must; and as staff requirements become more complex and diverse, planning must reach further and further into the future so that the required number of people with specialized training and experience will come on stream at the right times. Flexible-age retirement frustrates that kind of projection.

For the employee, inflation of course makes any kind of planning precarious. But even if inflation should be brought under control, flexible-age retirement has brought new hazards that offset such attractions as it might have.

And there are attractions. In spite of the hazards I have cited, we should not dismiss the plus values of opportunities for second careers or of being able to continue working into older years. Both for their own financial and physical well-being and for a more productive society, people should be encouraged to remain active in one way or another as long as they are able.

Bounced—but Still Bouncing

Q Could you discuss some of the special problems of executives—including CEOs—who lose their jobs? What are the more common reasons why they are fired?

A It is estimated that 100,000 executives are fired every year. And the number is not likely to shrink in today's economic pattern. Even before the current recession began to put the squeeze on company profits and to put pressure on managements to trim the fat off payrolls, other forces were operating to make executives "redundant." The continuing wave of mergers and takeovers is the most obvious: who needs two treasurers, two marketing chiefs, or two controllers?

So many of these firings are not for cause, and are no reflection on the quality of the executive displaced.

Even without mergers, investor demand for "performance" and the public push for greater director accountability have put managements under pressure to exact maximum results out of every position. When this brings reshuffles in top commands, the resulting clashes of personalities are often resolved by the "displacement" (another of the new euphemisms coming into management language) of the low man on the totem pole.

I shall deal later with some of the steps that are being taken by companies to help those discharged to land on their feet elsewhere. But first, a word about those who have brought their firing on themselves may help others like them to avoid a similar fate. Even though they too may be given the same kind of help in relocation, it is not a welcome experience.

Executives are let out for an infinite variety of reasons, which can often be described as failure to meet their corporate goals. But digging down deeper, executive-search and other consultants report that the most common single basic reason is failure in people relations.

And this failure occurs all the way to the top. Not all of the 100,000 executives who lose their jobs are subordinates, fired by the CEO. Some of them are the CEOs themselves, who are terminated by their boards of directors (thus debunking the myth that all boards of directors are captives of management).

What prompts a board to fire its CEO? It is a solemn undertaking, probably the most painful that a board is ever called upon to do. The very fact—in apparent support of the myth—that many of them have been handpicked by management only makes it more painful for the directors to take an ouster action. But in today's climate of director accountability and legal liability, boards do act when they are convinced that the best interest of the company demands it.

CEOs, like their subordinates, are discharged for many specific reasons. These usually add up to failure in the CEO role as such; and that in turn has usually involved some failure in people relations.

One executive after another who has performed brilliantly in a functional role and has risen through all the levels to the top of his field—be it marketing, production, finance, or whatever—has fallen apart when he got the total responsibility of running the whole company. It is an oversimplification to call it the Peter Principle at work. He has not necessarily reached his level of incompetence; but he may have reached a level where he has not been able emotionally, temperamentally, or intellectually to cope with the sheer variety and volume of new conceptual demands, or to keep all his priorities straight.

More often, though, he has failed in some aspect of people management.

A glaring example has been in the press recently of a man who had been outstanding in his handling of a succession of larger and larger functional responsibilities, including finally building the company's international operations to new heights of profitability. Then he was made CEO and the company almost immediately began to lose ground, both in market share and in profits. By the time his board realized that the mounting losses were no mere temporary deviation, he had also lost some 200 key executives from the company, including several of his most senior backup officers. The directors had discounted the first two or three defections as reflecting only disappointment at his having edged them out of the competition for the top job. But when they began an investigation in depth, they found that from the moment he had come to full power, he had revealed traits he had kept carefully concealed on his way to the top. One after another senior officer interviewed by members of the board reported the same thing: that he had repeatedly humiliated and denigrated them in the presence of others. In the process he had destroyed whatever motivation his associates might have had to work with him in building a strong company.

The Care and Feeding of Founders

Q I have noticed that the CEO who directly succeeds the founder of a company while the founder is still alive seems to run into special problems. Sometimes those problems are fatal—the job mortality among these successors seems pretty high. Is there a reason for that, and is there anything the successor can do to improve his chances of survival?

A For an object lesson in what to do and what not to do when taking over the top command of a company from the man who founded it, consider two cases, one involving a large airline and the other a large regional bank. In both cases, the eventual successor was brought in from the outside.

The top two officers of the airline were the actual founder and his most trusted, closest associate who had been second in command from the first day.

Once elevated to the top, the new airline chief showed his independence by totally ignoring the founder and this associate except when he met them in meetings of the board of direc-

134

tors—and even then he would rudely brush aside any suggestions or comments either of them would make in meetings.

He followed the same tactics with other executives who had been close to the founder and his associate. He was less receptive to recommendations or suggestions from them than from others in the company—as if he were afraid that he might become the captive of the older group.

Throughout the company it had been no secret that the airline's earnings had been slipping, and that the original management had lost much of its grip on operations. But there was tremendous loyalty to the founder; and when the word got around that the founder and his closest lieutenants were getting cavalier treatment, there was widespread resentment. The new boss got minimum, nominal cooperation—but no more.

The troubles of the airline were sufficiently deep-seated that with the best of managerial skill and the greatest of cooperation from everyone else, the new executive would have had enough difficulty in turning the company around. But this man failed dismally. When he made mistakes, no one rushed forward to rescue him—they just let him make the mistakes. And the mistakes began to add up to very poor performance until finally, after a relatively brief tenure, he was dismissed from the company.

The banker, meanwhile, followed exactly the opposite course. He actually had a more difficult job to do, because he was setting about virtually to revolutionize the bank. He was injecting not only new banking ideas, but a highly different personal style of management.

He organized the bank from top to bottom; he even changed the name of the bank. He retired or displaced some "old standby" employees.

But he did all this with the support of his predecessor and most of that man's host of friends—and largely because of his approach. Early in his stay in the chief executive job, he went to his predecessor and said in effect, "Everyone does things differently and looks at things a little differently. You would want me to be myself and use by best judgment, or you would not have hired me. You won't always like or approve of what I'm doing, but I always want you to know what I'm planning, and above all why I'm planning it. You may want to talk me out of some of my ideas, and I hope you will always try to do it if you don't agree with me; because even when you don't change my decision, you may help me avoid pitfalls I hadn't seen, and keep me from going off half-cocked."

It worked, and is continuing to work, just that way. The younger man has rarely abandoned completely any plan that he had developed and reviewed with the older one; but he has often made modifications based on some piece of new information or new insight that the older man could give him. Meanwhile the older man has gained increasing respect for his successor, and has sung his praises in all his own circles throughout the community.

While the newer man would eventually have made it on his own because he is a genuinely able person, his progress was speeded up immeasurably because he was so immediately accepted in places where there might have been resistance if his predecessors and his close friends had shown any antagonism or mistrust.

Meanwhile the older man has been shown the respect he deserves, has been made to feel appreciated both inside the bank and out, and has helped to present to the public an image of a united front that is a much better business developer for a bank than an atmosphere of dissension.

The key ingredients in any succession to top command—but especially when succeeding the founder—are maturity and confidence enough in your own judgment and sense of direction that you do not have to be afraid to listen to suggestions from others; humility enough to recognize that your predecessor must have had some great strengths or he could not have built what he did; and practical wisdom enough to know that it is better to have the founder's support than his opposition as long as you do not have to compromise your own integrity.

Outplacement—Help for When the Ax Falls

Q I understand that some new and special services have sprung up to help those discharged to land on their feet. What are they?

A Concern over the displacement of people has led to the creation in recent years of a new professional service to business with the elegant name of "outplacement." At first blush it might sound like a euphemism—a fancy name for kicking people out the door. But it is much more than that.

When it becomes apparent that an executive is not measuring up to what is expected of him, and management has concluded that there is no hope of either improvement on that job or greater success on another assignment, then the next question is how to handle the separation. The outplacement service has been developed to help those discharged to make the move from one job to another with a minimum of economic loss and a minimum of emotional damage. Whether the motivation is humanitarian, to help the displaced executive and his family weather the storm, or utilitarian, to ease the trauma of the management that has to do the firing, is perhaps beside the point. What does seem certain is that the result is usually better than it would have been under the common pattern in which the executive was given his walking papers and left to fend for himself.

While the details may vary, the major outplacement firms all operate on essentially the same principle: recognition that no matter how much the executive may realize that he is skating on thin ice (and many do not realize it at all), he is seldom prepared for the traumatic moment when the boss breaks the news that he is fired. So he is likely to be in some degree of shock and, in that state of shock, to do something impulsive and damaging to his own prospects.

So one of the first objectives of outplacement is to keep the discharged person from making any of several wrong moves. Only after that come the second and later objectives: to help him make a succession of right moves.

In a typical situation, the outplacement counselor will be waiting in a closed room near the office where the terminal interview is going on. Then, before the victim can get to a telephone to blurt out the bad news even to his own wife, let alone a talkative friend or a newspaper reporter, and before he can go out and get drunk—or worse—he is taken into the room where the consultant is waiting for him. There, behind closed doors, several things happen. He has a chance to blow off steam ("to ventilate his anger" is the professional euphemism) in a place where he cannot damage any future prospects. If he had been given time to do that in the boss's office, the reasoning goes, he might have launched into bitter personal attacks that would have shut off any possibility of the boss later giving him favorable references.

Then he will be counseled by a skilled professional on every aspect of his situation: his immediate mental and emotional state, the frame of mind in which he must approach his next placement or career steps, and what he must do to prepare himself for the most effective next contacts—preparation of resumes, possible advertisements, etc.

Later he will be counseled not only by the original consultant but by a team of two or three who will guide him on all the followup steps.

None of the major outplacement firms act as executive-search or placement consultants, to find the new job for the client. As one consultant says, "One of our principal objectives is to preserve or restore the client's self-confidence. If we find his job for him, we weaken that. We want to show him how *he* can do it—and we do." Another reason is inherent in the fact that executive-search firms do not handle outplacement assignments. As the president of the Association of Executive Recruiting Consultants has said, "Our association's ethical code prevents search firms from working both sides of the street, to avoid potential conflicts of interest."

(Incidentally, while I have referred to the individual as the client, the discharging company is the actual client, paying all the fees. These will run from 10 to 15% of the discharged executive's annual salary.)

The outplacement firms claim a remarkably high success rate. Their aim is to have their candidates back at work within six months, and they say that 80 to 85% are successful within that time—the higher-paid jobs taking longer. (One firm has a rule of thumb that allows at least one week for each $2,000 of annual salary.)

Moreover, it is claimed, 50 to 60% end up in better-paying jobs than they lost. One firm claims that 40% make "lateral" moves—salary equal to what they had before; only 8% are said to end in lesser jobs, and 2% to drop out without concluding the process.

Termination is not the only event that triggers the need for outplacement counseling: there is also the relocation problem. Many employees resist moving from one location to another, especially if they have working spouses who will have to leave their jobs.

So some companies have provided outplacement counseling to these spouses, offering them training in how to find employment in the new location. The aim, of course, is to enable the company employee to move without worrying about the loss of family income from the spouse's becoming unemployed.

VII

Harnessing the Energy: Organization

If people are the power plant of a company and if leadership is the spark plug, the ignition system, that fires that power plant, there still has to be a transmission system that delivers that power and converts it into work.

That transmission system is the organization of the company. It is more than just the organization *structure*, although it includes structure. It embodies all the several elements by which the energies, talents, and skills of large numbers of people are harnessed, concentrated, and focused on getting the best results.

It has to be a continuing concern of the executive. It is how he gets "from here to there"—from an idea to a result.

Building Your Team

Q My company manufactures components for computerized systems used in industrial-process controls. Until recently I have been able to oversee the entire operation, with every department and division head reporting directly to me. Now we have so many units and are spread over so much geography that it is impossible for me to keep tabs on everything. I know I have to revamp my organization, and turn over much of the top-level responsibility—and authority—to one or more executives. Much as I hate it, I'm resigned to having a layer or two between me and the unit heads.

But my question is, What kind of an organization should we have? Should it be highly centralized, or should it be decentralized? If decentralized, should we be organized on geographic lines, or by industry groupings? And how many people should I have reporting to me? Are there any functions I should still have reporting direct to me?

A There is no single, sacred pattern of organization to fit every company. The needs of each company are special to that company, and the organization should be tailored to those needs as well as to your management style. Furthermore, I never saw a company succeed or fail solely because of its organization structure. Other factors weigh so heavily that a company can succeed in spite of the most absurd of organization patterns, or fail with a textbook model.

The bank with which I was associated operated for many years under a structural plan that defied all the rules of organization planning and theory—and defied any attempt to justify it on logical or rational grounds. Yet other qualities inherent in the management—innovation, creativity, momentum, high-quality leadership—overrode the theoretical (and some genuine) organizational shortcomings.

But a good pattern of relationships—for supervision, for communication and expediting, for reporting and accountability —can facilitate your operation. A poor structure can do real damage and inhibit growth. So the time when you are compelled to revamp your structure may be an ideal moment to build in as many "energizers" as possible and knock out all the stumbling blocks you can spot.

Every element of your plan has to be decided on the basis of *your* peculiar set of facts. There are, however, a few rules of thumb that you can use to test each of your decisions.

First, the geographic vs. functional question: If your company has constant dealings with large numbers of individuals at every level of community life—customers, local governments, schools, political and civic leaders—geographic grouping may be necessary. Financial institutions, retailers, and service companies tend to need structures based on local and regional lines. But for a manufacturing company, a functional or industry grouping usually makes more sense.

A tougher decision to make is how far to centralize or decentralize.

Again, some rules of thumb will suggest where to start. You will have the greatest momentum and efficiency when every level of your operation—and every individual at every level—has the maximum degree of authority and autonomy that he can be safely trusted to use. Your aim is to hold to a minimum the number of times that people must come upstream for approvals, as well as the number of reporting layers between the action and the point of decision. You have to plan hard against building in bureaucratic delays.

That means good followup through monitoring and reporting, so that you can always know how well your people are performing without getting in their way by constantly looking over their shoulders. Even before that, it means good selection and training of people at every level.

Many CEOs and their organization planners agonize over how to strike the right balance between not having too many layers of supervision and not having the span of control of any one executive be greater than he can handle effectively. Both problems are related to how well the company has pushed responsibility and authority outward and downward throughout the organization.

It is appalling how often companies violate the basic rule of efficiency: that every task should be performed by the most junior person who can handle it competently. By this ideal, the number of layers can be shrunk dramatically.

At the same time, each supervisor can handle a vastly wider span of control if everybody below him has maximum authority along with his responsibility. The supervisor then can spend more time in monitoring and evaluating performance, because he spends less time making "transactional" decisions that somebody below him should be making.

Among management no-no's, the worst is the "one-on-one" layer of supervision at any level. A supervisor has just one subordinate reporting to him, and looking to him for decisions.

So absurd does this scheme seem that it might be supposed that no one would ever be so foolish as to set up such a line of command. But it happens surprisingly often.

A one-on-one pair usually reflects management's lack of confidence in either of the people, plus a mistaken assumption that persons who are considered inadequate will somehow bolster each other enough to equal one good link in the chain of operation. What usually results in such situations is chronic bottlenecking as the papers shuffle back and forth awaiting decisions.

There still is the question of how much of the decision making is going to keep coming up to you, and how much gets done somewhere short of you.

You must make up your mind that you are going to let someone else make many of the final decisions that you've been in the habit of making. At first that "someone else" might be just one person: your next in command, ideally a person who has the potential to succeed you some day. In any case, it must be someone who can stand in for you in your absence, and who needs all the broadening and testing you can give him.

So how do you and he or she divide the show between you? In part it depends on your respective strengths and weaknesses; but in general, you should keep under your wing all the things that might be called "corporate": finance, legal, public relations including any legislative or governmental relations you might have, and personnel.

Your deputy should be able to keep his eye on all the operations that are involved in getting the raw materials in one door and finished goods out the other on schedule and at minimum cost. You pick an operations boss and retain policy control.

If he lacks background in sales or marketing so that you have to help in that area, try to do it in a way that leaves him enough clout to be able to step in to break the bottleneck between sales and production. That's the likeliest place to find a drag on profits, and if you aren't careful you will be the drag.

Organization Patterns— or Principles?

Q You have written that there is no single, sacred pattern that fits every company and that each company must tailor its own. But are there any guiding principles that would help us to shape our plan?

A There are checklists, but most of the "guiding principles" cannot be absolute because there are so many variables. Differences in size and complexity of businesses dictate quite different organization plans. Most successfully managed companies have gone through a succession of organization changes —centralized, less centralized, functional, product, geographic, and many others.

So one of the first principles should be flexibility—be prepared not only to change from time to time, but to keep units simple enough and flexible enough to preserve the entrepreneurial spirit.

Second, remember: structure is not organization. Don't start with structure as your first concern. That will emerge out of several other things you look at first.

Third, if you don't start with structure, where do you start? One practitioner in organization planning says, "The most basic thing to remember is, What is the mission? It is to produce a product or service, and to have it purchased by customers at a profit. The aim of an organization plan is to ensure that those two things happen with the least delay, interference, or duplication of effort."

A group at McKinsey & Company identified seven major factors which, for ease of memory, they alliterated into seven S's:

Structure
Strategy
Systems
Style
Skills
Staff
Superordinate goals

But in their illustrative chart, they clustered the other six around the *goals* as the central focus of the approach to productive organization change—just as the practitioner quoted above cited the "mission." The first six they consider of such equal importance that none can be overlooked, nor any one or two allowed to override the others.

What they mean by each of these six factors is spelled out in the June 1980 issue of *Business Horizons*.

Participative—or Not

Q I hear and read a lot about "participative management" and I am bothered by it. How can I, as manager, let people participate by providing inputs without their expecting to share in the deciding? I have to make the ultimate decision on the real management problems, but I can't help being concerned about "agreement" or "consensus" if I have invited participation.

A Buzzwords like "participative," "consensus," and "democracy in business" can mean so many different things to different people that they can lead to fuzzy thinking and misconceptions. Without debating any of the current management theory, let me recite a few convictions and then suggest a few things that can and should be done.

When I say that business cannot be managed by consensus, I do not mean that no one's views but the manager's should be heard or listened to.

When I say that managing a company is not a democratic process, neither do I mean that the manager must be autocratic in his conduct or attitudes.

I mean simply that business is managed by a series of decisions made by a pyramid of individuals who take final responsibility for their decisions and for the consequences of them.

That still leaves plenty of room for participation and sharing, at every level. But I don't like to put a label on it, like "participative management" or "management by consensus"; in fact, I like to avoid labels for this kind of management activity, because labels encourage acting by formula—and that is dangerous. If I had to put a label on it, I would call it "participative *leadership*" rather than "*management*," because it has to do with a manager's style more than any structure or process of management.

But putting a label on it implies that it is a policy or concept that is going to be applied companywide and top to bottom. That is precisely what should not be done. It has to be applied selectively, in places where it will work and with people who can make it work.

No manager in a company of any size can do everything or know all about everything. So the wise manager involves as many people as he can at every level in both work and decision making. He follows the basic rule that every task should be done by the most junior person who can handle it competently; and he includes in that rule its corollary, that decision-making authority should also be pushed out as close to the scene of the action as experience will justify.

Many operations, for example in the plant community where a number of workers are doing the same or related tasks, lend themselves to some real group decision sharing. In matters of safety or working conditions—anything affecting the workers' physical well-being—they clearly should have a voice. Even beyond that, although the responsible supervisor has to decide *what* they are to do, the workers themselves often have a better sense of *how* to do it. As Peter Drucker has pointed out, what matters is that self-government of plant-community tasks be local self-government, and that it put the responsibility where the consequences of the decisions have to be lived with.

Such a self-governing work community is not "participatory democracy" because the working teams are organized by management for specific operations and specific jobs.

There finally are some decisions that the top man cannot buck down to anyone else; he must make them on his own. But he can listen. And the wise manager does listen—selectively. Just as the chief executive has to select the people to whom he delegates decision-making authority, so does the wise manager select the people he will listen to—not necessarily the same people on each issue.

Once in a while, when new ground is being explored and the ingredients of the problem are not clearly defined, the executive may find it effective to consult his advisers as a group. I have seen a good leader orchestrate such a probing discussion so skillfully that the group itself, by examining and discarding alternatives, arrived at the only possible conclusion, which the executive accepted as his decision. But they knew, and he knew, that it was *his* decision, because at any moment he could have rejected any part of it that he disapproved. That should be made plain by the manner of your approach, whether in one-to-one discussion or in a group: that you welcome and respect their views, but that you may have to take other considerations into account.

This leads to one cardinal rule which, added to the paragraph above, helps to answer your questions: again, whether singly or in groups, whenever you make a decision that is not entirely in line with the advice you have received, tell the others why you decided as you did. The unforgivable sin is to invite advice, ignore it, and not give the adviser the dignity of an explanation.

To fail to listen is bull-headed; to accept everything you hear is naive. Good management organization involves selecting for every level people mature enough to know when to listen and when to act.

Participative Projects Pay Off

There are many one-shot "participative" projects in a company that I didn't mention above. They can involve people at many different levels, letting them participate in developing plans, making decisions, and executing programs—experiences they might not have a chance to be exposed to in the normal course of their regular duties.

The best of these opportunities are indeed projects—something outside the regular flow of operations. The kind of off-the-line-of-traditional-promotion assignment I mentioned earlier as useful in reintroducing returnees will fit here—studies of proposed acquisitions, new products, new processes, etc. But the fast-changing area of environmental, consumer, and other social-policy pressures on companies offers a whole new field for involving officers and employees in group action. Promising junior people can analyze problems and issues to prepare recommendations for more senior action; and since many of these problem areas are new, unplowed ground with no established policy, they lend themselves to the kind of interdepartmental consulting that generates a feeling of participating.

I saw this whole process demonstrated in one continuing chain of events in our bank. After the Watts riots of 1965, when the ghetto areas and decaying inner cores of many of our cities were centers of appalling social problems, it was plain that any company with roots as deep in the community as our bank's had to do more than was being done to help find solutions. The question was where to start. Instead of calling in a consulting firm or looking to some agency of government for guidance, the bank detached two young M.B.A.s, who had completed their first tour of duty in the bank and were ready for their next assignment, and turned them loose as a task force. Their only job description was that they were not to come back until they could present to management a concrete recommendation as to what the bank could and should do on this urban problem. Their report was so complete and precise that it became the foundation for everything the bank undertook and is still doing in its urban affairs department.

Then when that department became part of an even broader social-policy committee program, every major department of the bank became involved. A whole network of task forces was put to work researching public issues and bank practices impinging on the public interest.

In the meanwhile I saw another task force of two bright young officers tackle the problem of how to recycle the mountains of paper that pass through a bank. Not only did they develop a recycling program that was a credit to the bank, but I am told that it had repercussions far beyond the bank. They learned enough about the logistics of how to collect paper in a large organization that other kinds of companies all over the country asked for copies of their report so that they could adapt the process to their operations. On top of that, this young task force had laboratory tests made on possible additional uses of re-cylced paper that caused the paper industry to revise some of its previous assumptions.

Involvement in these off-pattern issues was a tremendously broadening experience for the task-force members and gave a great boost to creative and innovative interests. It also gave management a chance to observe and test these young people in new settings. Even for the more senior officers, the involvement introduced many into new areas of public-policy participation.

If the task-force assignment is going to require full time, the ideal time to make it is when the employee is ready to leave one job and move on to another, so that there is a minimum of career interruption.

People Who Can Steer
You Straight

Q My problem is personal but it can affect my effectiveness for my company as well as for myself. I have recently taken a new job in a different company—head of a major department. All the working conditions I was promised have materialized. But I find myself at a disadvantage with my peers who have been around for years and know all the "rabbit trails"—whom to call for what service, where to find the right answers to any kind of internal problem. What's the best way to learn the "off-paper" organization of a company?

A There is no single best way, but there are a lot of things that usually work. They all involve an old adage, "To make a friend, don't do him a favor; ask him to do you a favor." Nobody is likely to feel anything but complimented by being asked for advice.

But before you start asking everyone willy-nilly—and maybe getting some bum steers—let me suggest a course of action. The one person in your company who has a vested interest in seeing that you succeed and prosper is the man who hired you—your CEO or whoever. He also is the most likely to know the right and wrong sources of help. You should not hesitate to go to him and say, in effect, "I know how to find my own answers on my job itself; but it will get me up to speed months sooner if I know where to turn for all the dozens of little support services and, above all, for guidance on how to get things done through the company machinery. Who is a wheel horse who knows his way around, and who can be depended on to steer me straight?"

Every well-managed company has one or more such wheel horses, and your chief will know who yours is. There are plenty of others in your company who would be glad to have you coming to them for help, but whose advice would for various reasons lead you into a booby trap. Your chief can help you avoid those.

Another kind of help you should ask your chief to get you, if you don't already have it: a mature, competent secretary who will keep you from stubbing your toe on all kinds of internal—and much external—folklore and practice: how to spell and pronounce people's names, what their nicknames are if any, even the correct names or common designations of departments and sections of the company that someone might be touchy about, not to speak of traffic-managing you so that you keep a good reputation by getting to appointments on time in distant parts of the building or the community. Such an associate can be priceless, and you should not settle for second best.

Knowing the "Rabbits"
Is the CEO's Job

Q Forty lashes with a wet noodle for saying a CEO should be bothered with such things as the "rabbit trails" for getting things done when a secretary can handle it better and faster and make her boss shine even brighter!"

A I thought that I had acknowledged the importance of the secretary in this whole introductory-adjustment process; but on rereading I find that I did put most of my emphasis on just a part of the secretarial value. That was not intended to limit her contribution only to those items. She might even be the one the CEO would recommend as the most reliable guide.

But I still would caution against taking it for granted that a secretary is automatically the right person to look to for all kinds of "rabbit-trail" guidance. Just as there are executives and executives, so that you should pick and choose carefully, so there are secretaries and secretaries. Many who are superb in every other respect would be miscast in this role.

As for the CEO being bothered, this is a perfectly appropriate part of his job—yet one that can be done with a minimum of effort and a maximum of yield.

161

VIII

Managing with Information

Even though management is the art of making decisions on the basis of less than complete information, information is, paradoxically, at the heart of good decision making. The question is, What information? Modern technology has produced an information explosion; the debris could bury management if it is not sifted and sorted.

Offered here are some guidelines for that kind of screening, to the end that information may accelerate management's momentum—not paralyze it.

Management Information Systems

Q We have been using a computer for some of our own accounting, controls, and other data processing; but we have never tried to develop a real information system. Now the staff people who run our data processing are pushing to have us install a real management information system, not only developing our own data base but tying into some other computer-based data sources.

They make a strong case for what such a system would do for us, not only in better management control of our own operations but in better insight into markets, competition, and economic trends as a guide to our business planning.

But I find the size of this proposal a little staggering: the cost of installing it, the cost of keeping it up, and the question whether we are really geared up to make effective use of what the system would deliver to us. I may be falling behind the parade, but I'm a little frightened by the project. Should I be?

A Frightened, no; but concerned, yes.

You should take a good, thorough look at everything your staff is proposing, and at all the other pros and cons of such information flows. There is no doubt that business runs on information today to a degree we never dreamed of a generation ago.

But you put your finger on the most central question: are you geared up to make effective use of what the system would deliver to you? I put that ahead of your two cost questions—and those are not minor issues. You can take as a rule of thumb that information you use productively will repay its cost, while information you do not use not only is a wasted cost, but can impose an added burden of hidden cost just by being around.

This hidden cost is like many others in business: the time spent in nonproductive activity, and the consequent distraction from essential efforts. In this case the distraction is the burden of wading through bales of irrelevant data just because they have been labeled as "information pertinent to the management of the business."

You, the CEO, are not the only one who might get so distracted—that is not where the hidden cost comes in. You might be able to take care of yourself, just by ignoring what you didn't want to be bothered with. But many of the others down the line who are wired into the system might not feel so free to pick and choose—or might not want to confess their inadequacy in not being able to figure why they are being sent all these reports.

I am starting off with the negatives, without being at all negative about the basic idea. I do it for a good reason: you should use these negatives as your test, your check points, from the very first discussion of a system. You should compel those advocating the system to satisfy you with the answer to each of the questions.

There is nothing new about these hazards—imaginatively new as many of the pluses are. Since long before anyone coined the term "management information system," businesses have been plagued with excessive flows of reports and data. The new electronic technology has simply multiplied the opportunities for both good and bad explosions of data.

Too much of the information that flows to the CEO either is a by-product of routine paperwork processing or is what some functional unit has an interest in feeding to top management. In either case, an overwhelming mass of data is likely to cross the executive's desk—none of it addressed to his *real* needs, or even to what he had perceived as his needs.

Much of it is only what someone else had perceived as his needs. Or, nowadays, it is what has evolved as a "management information system"—with everything in it but the kitchen sink.

So where should you start in considering what, if anything, to include in such a system? The first answer is, Don't start with the data.

Start at the other end. Start by looking at your job, and asking yourself what kinds of information would help you do it better; and ask each of your management team who would be wired into this system to do the same thing. Each of them will have—or should have—a different answer, because their needs are different.

Management Functions Supported by Information Systems

Q What have you to say about the kinds of management function that can be supported by information, and about how the different levels of management make different uses of information?

A In general, there are two kinds of management function that can be supported by information: business building and monitoring. These can be extended or subdivided infinitely, but most uses of data are to support one of these two management purposes. Either you are analyzing how you can penetrate more of your present market or some new market or can enter into a new line of business, and you want to know all you can know about the markets, competition, required investment, and expected return on investment, or you want to know how your company, and each of its divisions, has been doing on your present operations.

Everything you want to know about the whole company each of your division heads wants to know about the operations he is responsible for. And as you go further down the scale, the emphasis shifts from projection of business plans to more and more monitoring, until the lowest supervisor on the information circuit would be monitoring only the performance of individuals in his unit.

Obviously no two people in this entire information chain have identical information needs. They not only need different kinds of data, but they need data with different frequency and different timeliness.

To say that you will have a single management information system that will serve the needs of the whole company would be absurd unless you recognize that what you must have is a "system of systems."

So what you would need to know, for each user of information, is what kinds of data he will need, how often he will need each kind, and how promptly.

Then someone must calculate another kind of cost: not only the hardware and the people to run it, but what kind of burden will it put on the people who will be the sources of the data? How many new report forms will be needed? How much, if at all, will the supplying of data slow down the operation?

All these are part of the cost-benefit tradeoff. If you can be satisfied that the benefit exceeds the cost by the proper margin, you would not be a good manager if you did not go ahead.

Another new term has crept into the language of information: "decision-support information." Each piece of data that is collected and disseminated should be a useful support to a decision. And the cost-benefit data are among the pieces you should have to support your decision.

(As the term is coming to be used, decision-support information includes more than just data. Those working with the concept have been developing models to test the effects of alternate courses of action based on the data. But the term is useful even without the models.)

Another new term that introduces a helpful factor into the information-building process is "critical success factor" (CSF). This one involves the concept that in most industries there are just a few—usually from three to six—factors that determine success. These key jobs must be done exceedingly well for a company to be successful. If results are satisfactory in this limited number of areas, they are likely to ensure successful competitive performance for the company, even though some other areas may have lagged.

Conversely, there are a few areas where things *must* go right for the company to flourish. If results in these areas are not good enough, the company's total results will fall short.

This suggests both that information needed for successful performance be developed and used beforehand and that those supervising or monitoring the performance have the necessary information so that they can follow results closely—closely enough, and currently enough, that strategies could be revised if need be.

While the CSF approach was originally for the top executive's use in running the whole company, it can be just as useful at every level of management to which many functions report. It can help managers decide where they need to focus their greatest attention, both in planning and in performance evaluation.

By my raising of cautions, I would not suggest that you sell the management-information-systems people short. Some of them have learned things about the use of information that those of us who came up a more traditional route never knew existed. So listen to them—but don't be bullied by them. Consider calmly whether they have something to offer that you can learn to use profitably.

As for the question of whether it might be falling behind the parade to feel cautious in this area, be sure it is the competitive parade or the profit parade you are racing—not the fad parade.

If you will apply these tests you can screen out any fad elements and get down to solid management ingredients.

IX

The Lubricant of the Machine: Morale

To carry the automotive analogy one step further: if people are the power plant, if leadership is the spark plug, if organization is the transmission system—then morale is the lubricant that makes the whole machine run smoothly.

What morale is, how it is generated (and how it can be damaged), and how this lubricant is carried out to all the parts that would otherwise generate the heat of friction—all these have to be a major concern of the executive.

So closely related that it might be called the end product of a high-morale operation is an atmosphere of creativity and innovation. That too can be fostered and nurtured by the influence of the executive, or it can be choked to death.

The plus value, the extra dividends that can come from making the right choice, make this one of the high-yield facets of the art of being an executive.

Morale

Q Reports come to me (mostly via the grapevine) that the morale is poor in some of our plants and office units. The heads of those operations deny the rumors, but we have had an opinion survey made recently and it confirms the report.

I don't understand how it could be, and especially I don't understand why morale should be low in some parts of the company and high in others. We treat them all alike, and I think we treat them well. We have done everything we can think of to build good morale: we sponsor softball and basketball teams, we have company picnics, we created an employees' club that has dinner dances and other social events that we partially subsidize. All in all, we have tried to maintain a "happy family" atmosphere.

A If you equate company picnics with good employee morale, you have more of a problem than you thought you had. Not that there is anything wrong with company picnics, softball teams, or any of the other socializing that you have sponsored—nothing wrong, that is, if you do not force them down your employees' throats. But at best, all those social and athletic events do not get at the real root of the morale problem.

Morale is one of the most elusive concepts that a manager has to deal with, and it is one that can easily lead the manager astray. It is usually mixed up with the debate as to the better way to run a company or a department: as a "taut ship" or as a "happy ship." My experience and observation tell me that the taut ship, with high standards fairly administered, is always the happiest. Morale is always higher among workers who have high demands made upon them but are able to meet those demands—and are shown appreciation for meeting them—than among a group that work under sloppy supervision with low or no standards set for their performance.

What this suggests is that morale is related to pride in one's work and is a function of one's own sense of self-worth. If employees can feel pride in the place where they work so they don't have to apologize to their friends for working for that outfit, pride in their particular boss-supervisor, some sense of pride in the job they are assigned to do, and pride in the way they have performed that job, and feel that they have been appreciated in their job and their performance and that they are fairly compensated, then you are most likely to have good morale. If any of those is missing, morale is going to suffer.

And each of those six ingredients is manageable. In fact, each of them *has* to be managed, if you want consistently good results: you may accidentally get good marks in any or all of them from time to time without trying, but it is not safe to count on that. So let's look at them separately.

The first one—pride in the company—may be the most important and is certainly basic; but it is so all-encompassing that it would require several chapters (if not an entire book) to deal adequately with it.

But meanwhile, all the others are so specifically related to attitudes of individual employees that we can single them out and deal with them separately. First, pride in the immediate boss-supervisor: if the people who work in any unit know that their supervisor is unfair in his treatment of employees, if he is carrying on an affair with someone in the unit and everyone knows it, if he comes to work with a hangover or otherwise "goldbricks" on the job, if in any respect he is known to be incompetent or inadequate for his job, then the morale in his unit will be poor.

So first of all, look at the quality of your supervisors.

Then, even with otherwise competent supervisors, study how they introduce employees to their jobs and the details of their tasks. No matter how routine or assembly-line a job may be, it should be explained, not in terms of "Tighten this nut on this bolt" or "Put the pink slips here and the blue slips there," but in terms of "What you do holds the whole transmission in place, so it's important to the operation of the whole car." Or "This is the way we record the investments in our trust accounts. So what you do is very important in keeping our records straight and our customer accounts accurate."

Next, if they are to feel pride in their own performance, they need to know what is expected of them—what is "par for the course" in quantity and in quality, if that is measurable.

Then, if they have performed at or better than par, they need to feel that someone in authority has noticed that and appreciated it. They won't feel that if they don't hear it, right out loud—if their boss doesn't stop at his or her station periodically to say, "That's nice work."

Of course, if it isn't good work, that needs to be said too; but if that is the only time the boss is heard from, don't expect good morale. Even when the work is not up to par, the criticism should be aimed at trying to find the cause and helping the employee to improve—the boss should not just scold, threaten, or implant fear.

There may finally be no choice but to terminate, and the employee who is not improving should be warned that termination will be the next step; but if everyone in the unit is kept in constant fear of being fired, don't expect good morale there.

There are two schools of thought on the use of praise as a tool of management to encourage good performance. One school believes that praise spoils employees. I belong to the other school.

Finally, though, praise and appreciation do not pay the grocery bills. If employees feel they have done good work—and are told so by their bosses—and then are not paid what the market says that work is worth, the praise may even backfire as insincere softsoap. So while good morale can rarely be bought by money alone, neither can it be expected to flourish on skimpy pay rations.

Why is morale so important?

It is because morale and performance are so closely related. There can be individual exceptions—as with highly talented or self-motivated employees who are spurred into greater activity by the very circumstances that turn off the others. But it is a safe rule of thumb that productivity will be greater when morale, as I have defined it, is also higher.

Remember that morale always filters down from the top. It reflects the attitudes of people at every level—especially the attitudes of supervisors toward their own jobs and toward the people they supervise.

We like to think that we have good morale "from the ground up," and that is a good target to shoot for. But we don't really build it from the ground up. We have to defy all architectural principles by starting the building at the top—"hang it from sky hooks"—and building down until it reaches the ground.

Pull Up Your Socks
When Business Sags

Q My company is one of the so-called "structurally depressed" industries: too many manufacturers, too much production, flattened demand. Even though this moves in cycles in my industry, so that I know it will improve in time, it is hard to motivate employees in a period like this. They know that if they help us increase our productivity, they may only be speeding up the time when we will have to lay more people off. That has had a murderous effect on morale. Is there any way to counteract that and raise morale?

A It obviously is harder to generate high morale in a depressed industry than in one that is booming. Whether in sports, business, or war, people like to be on the winning side. The pride of identifying with the winner helps to produce a high, intense kind of morale; but because of its emotional content it also is perishable.

One thing is certain: any attempt to duplicate that state of euphoria by artificial or superficial tactics—any "cheerleader" kind of approach—is doomed to failure. Nothing but an honest, candid sharing of the facts will have any lasting impact. (I favor that approach in good times or bad, but in depressed times it is imperative.)

The factors that can be built into morale in the depressed industry are not the same as those that are effective in the booming industry—because the goals are different. (That is a point never to be forgotten in dealing with morale: solid, lasting morale must always be tied in with the goals of the organization; employees must understand at least the essentials of those goals and accept their part in them.)

The depressed industry cannot set greater production as its goal; but that does not suggest a psychology of despair. A company in that industry can have many goals that will be rallying points for pride of performance. Even in a cycle when the total market for the industry may have shrunk, somebody is going to sell *some* units of product; that can be an incentive to sharpen marketing and sales skills and approaches with a view to capturing a larger share of the market. Improving the quality of the product can still further enhance the market share, not only immediately but later when the market is larger.

Research and creativity may produce new uses of the product that will break through the limitations of the depressed market. Meticulous attention to delivery schedules and other aspects of customer service will help to cement present customer relations and build toward greater market share.

And, of course, at any level of output anything that can reduce the cost of production per unit will add to the net profit.

So a slack time is a time when everyone throughout the company can be enlisted in finding ways to "tidy up" the company: to sharpen and brighten its competitive performance in every department.

This approach will work only if the top man believes in it and commits the whole company to making it work.

Success in achieving any of these "pull up our socks" goals can give your people the same kind of pride of performance (which is at the heart of all solid morale) as any other kind of competitive success.

Loyalty—or Respect?

Q When our company was new, in the early part of this century, the workers had a strong loyalty to the company. Today's employees don't seem to have any of that feeling. Why is that?

A You say your employees don't show loyalty to your company the way early-day workers did. Are you sure that was loyalty, and not just fear? Heads of companies—especially founder-operators—used to speak of "my boys and girls," and employees acted out the part (they didn't tug their forelocks like feudal serfs, but they did tip their hats to the boss). But that didn't mean they were giving fealty to their lord and master.

Recent generations have seen workers gain a much greater sense of security and independence. They may have abused that in many ways, and they may not all have as much pride in personal skill and performance as workers did in a less mechanized day; but they have more self-respect in their relation to their employer. No employer can feel that he owns his workers, or that they "owe" him loyalty.

The very concept of loyalty suggests a kind of relationship that is out of key with the dignity with which today's workers (quite properly) expect to be treated. A boss—and a company—can expect to win *respect;* but even respect is something that has to be earned every day.

Four Steps of Communications (Part I)

Q In our management meetings I often hear someone say, "We do a lousy job of communications around here." They say they hear the same complaint from some subordinates. But they never tell me what we should do about it, until the other day one of them suggested that we should hire one of the consulting firms that specialize in communications to come in and study our problem, then lay out a program for us. Is that the way to go?

A I don't want to put the knock on consultants, because there are good ones in all fields, including this one. But in your case I think you should do a lot on your own before you call anyone else in. You haven't told me just what your real communications problem is. I wonder if you know. Remember the old rule: the first step is to define the problem. Most of the cases of bad communications I have seen had a few common ingredients. They add up to just four basic decisions that should have been made—and weren't. I call them my Four Steps of Communications.

The First Step of Communications is the decision to tell somebody something. Your board takes an action or you take an action, you decide to do something, you hire someone, or you have talked with a government official about one of your projects, or you have had a letter from someone, somewhere something has happened, or somebody has told you something—but it never occurs to you that somebody else might be interested, that someone else has a right to know, or that you would profit by letting someone else know. Right there is the first breakdown in communications.

Take a look at the word "communicate" and you will get a clue to what you are trying to do: it comes from the Latin *communicare* (to impact, to partake, to share). Not "from me down to you" or "you listen to me," but "together we share one problem, one set of facts, one understanding—one company." The key word in that last sentence is "share."

After you have decided that somebody else should know, Step Two is to decide who ought to know. Your department heads? All your employees? Your board of directors, or your shareholders? Or the whole plant community?

You should not be bashful about using any checklists and guides that will fit. Just as a homely little example: every person in the office who takes dictation should have a reminder sticker right on the cover of his or her notebook, with the simple question "Who should get a copy?" printed on it. And whoever takes the minutes of your meetings should also have a reminder, "Who should be told about this action?"

The third decision you must make is how much to tell them. The general answer to this one, Step Three, is "Tell them all they need or will be interested to know—but no more."

Here is where listening—inquiring—is important, especially in communicating with employees. In addition to employee opinion polls, surveys of employees' desires for information, and supervisors' inviting and answering questions, companies have used such other methods as advisory councils at various levels. A junior advisory council with rotating members from the youngest and lowest level of first-line supervision can be an effective way to tap the company grapevine.

And don't forget to tap your own memory. Before you became such a lofty big boss with your mind on stratospheric problems what were the things you and your buddies used to gripe about among yourselves? Most of them may have been taken care of by now. But if you're not sure, you might meet with your junior advisory council. Even if those particular complaints have now evaporated, your willingness to ask about them will open up a lot of talk about what is bothering people today.

One little special area of communications: when we tell our employees of a new rule, or of a new practice that we have adopted, so often we spell out meticulously what we are going to do, and how we are going to do it—and even worse, what and how we expect them to do things—but we don't bother to explain why.

Ten words of why can be worth 100 words of how.

Four Steps of Communications (Part II)

Q In our last chapter I began to respond to a reader who shared a common problem: "We do a lousy job of communications around here." The first step is to decide that you are going to share information. Second, decide who ought to know. Third, determine what or how much you are going to tell them; in order to do this . . .

A Companies have devised many ways to "look inside their employees' heads" to see what is currently bugging them and to see what they would like to know about the company that nobody is telling them. Employee attitude and opinion polls are not new, but companies have been learning a lot about how to conduct them. (This is one area where you might profit by some professional guidance.)

Not everything that employees want to know—or that they want to tell you—is of the kind that they would bring up in a survey or that you would include in a published report. Some of the most important things are those that come up in face-to-face contact right on the job. Not many of your employees have

188

direct access to you (although you should try never to brush them off, but to give them whole answers when they do contact you!). Most of their questions or comments are going to be given to supervisors somewhere in between them and you. You will need to make those supervisors realize that part—a large part—of their job is to be the two-way recorder and transmitter.

Whether by mass survey or face-to-face contact, you must be prepared for a lot of questions you never dreamed of answering before. This is not as big a shock as it would have been a few years ago, because disclosure is more nearly the order of the day now. SEC rulings have required disclosure of information that once would have been unthinkable to reveal, and some companies go beyond the requirements.

After you have decided what should be told, who should be told, and how much, it is relatively simple to take Step Four: to decide how to tell them. And yet I suspect that this is the part of communications that most of the time has been spent on. We spend a lot of time and money figuring out whether to do things in two colors or four, whether to do it by direct mail or through other media, whether to use art or not—and so on and so on. I am not belittling the importance of these fine points. But if we worry about those before we worry about whether we are saying the right things to the right people at the right time, we have put the cart before the horse. If we could always be sure that we were talking to people only about the things that they should know about and that we were telling them all the things they should know, it wouldn't matter too much how we said it.

No one can give you a formula that will tell you which things should be communicated in a mimeographed bulletin and which things in a printed piece, which ones should go in a personal letter and which ones in a form letter, which ones should be in writing at all and which ones should be delivered in person. But again, perhaps some questions will suggest their own answers:

Is the information so interesting to the people who get it that they want it right now and to heck with the fancy trimmings? In other words, will the mimeograph job do the trick for this group? Or does it need a little special treatment to attract attention and interest? Or is it of such major importance that it deserves to be dignified by even more special treatment in the way of printing, typography, choice of papers, and so on?

Is there someone who will be getting this communication who has a right to expect that it will be personally addressed to him? Or—whether he has a right to expect it or not—is there someone who would appreciate it enough to make it worth the trouble to write him a personal letter? Who are the ones who should be confronted face to face with an orally delivered message?

In this step, as in each of the other communications steps, the answers come fairly easily if we just ask ourselves the right questions. Again let me stress that the common failure in communications is the failure to ask ourselves any of these questions at all.

As you take each of the four steps in communicating, constantly remind yourself that it is a two-way street. Listening to others is one of the powerful processes for winning them over to your own point of view. If you won't stop to listen to the other person's viewpoint, you'll rarely convert him or her to your own. So-called "downward communication" works, because it focuses only on what we want to get across, not what the other person is interested in hearing or even able to perceive and understand.

Two Ears—One Mouth

Q The communications in our company don't seem to be working very well, and I can't figure why not. We have what we thought was a quite complete spread of publications and other forms of communicating with our employees: a home organ, departmental newsletters, bulletin boards, periodic letters on special topics, motion-picture and slide presentations for staff meetings, etc. Yet we have constant evidence that our message is not getting around. What are we missing?

A In your letter you recited a long list of the things you do to communicate with your employees, but there was one thing I didn't see anywhere in the list: I didn't see anything about *you* listening to *them.*

It is an old saw, but still true: God gave you two ears and only one mouth, and you should use them in that proportion. That is not just a cute saying. It has pointed meaning in company communications, for at least two reasons: If you are not doing *some* listening—some organized, careful listening—you have no way of knowing whether you are telling the employees the things they really want and need to know. And if you don't listen afterward, you won't know whether the things you told them really sank in: whether you told them in words they could understand, and in terms of ideas that are close to their interests.

Sperry Corporation, by the way, has recently published an excellent little booklet entitled *Your Personal Listening Profile* that is aimed at a broader spectrum of listening but still has some relevance to this part of employee communications. It is available on request.

Communicating—
One at a Time

Q I have reread your columns on communications and found them very helpful. But they touched only briefly on communicating with one employee at a time, about that person's own job, and what he or she needs to know in order to do it well. Maybe that isn't "communications" as you were dealing with it there; but it is an important problem for me as a supervisor. Can you add anything on that kind of communicating—whatever you call it?

A Indeed that is "communications," and more important than most of the things we do under that heading. I had dealt with it briefly in an earlier chapter concerned with morale; but it is so central that it deserves more complete treatment on its own.

If the goal of all employment is greater productivity, then that goal translates into greater contribution by each employee. And if, as I believe, employees make their greatest contribution when they know just what is expected of them and feel that they know just how to perform in order to deliver what is expected of them, when they, further, feel that they have been appreciated when they have performed well—or even have been corrected helpfully when they have not performed properly—then there is a whole chain of communication that management cannot afford to short-change.

Yet that chain is often neglected.

One reason is that is has to be preceded by another chain of communication of a different kind: the training of the supervisors who are going to supervise the final work. Too often the supervisor is not trained for supervision at all—he is simply assigned to it. And he views it in the literal sense of the word "supervise"—"to oversee," and by extension "to enforce performance." He should be trained—and modern preparation for supervision stresses this—to know that a basic part of his job is to be a teacher and a communicator.

Part of this teaching may be done by film or other audio-visual techniques, and to groups at a time. But excellent as many of these training films are, it still is the job of the supervisor to deal with employees one at a time and on the job: to be sure that each one understands everything the film was trying to say and feels comfortable and adequate in doing the job. If not, the supervisor has to straighten out the kinks. If the film is a good one, it covers the why as well as the how of each process; if it doesn't or if the point is not clear to the employee, the supervisor again has an interpreting job.

Where there is no such film, of course, the whole teaching job belongs to the supervisor—not just to say "Put the pink slips here and the blue slips there" and "Copy from this line of the slips to that line of this big sheet of paper" and "Tell the customer to fill out this form and take it over there," but to make sure the employee knows *why* each of these things is to be done. The employee needs to know just why each of these steps is important: what it does for the customer or what it does for the company—or both.

The employee needs to know, too, how his or her performance is going to be rated: what is going to determine whether a good job is being done or not.

All of that has to be said, right out loud, by the supervisor to each employee. It needs to be said at the outset, and it needs to be said again at the time that the performance is being rated. Especially if part of the performance has to be criticized (and corrected), it is important that any good performance is recognized and singled out for mention.

There is a school of thought that does not believe in the use of praise in supervision. I do not belong to that school. Praise has to be used with complete honesty and sincerity. But properly used, it is one of the effective tools of management.

Invest Wisely in Beauty

Q We are building a new building that will house all our headquarters functions, and I am chairman of a management committee to coordinate the project. We are trying to get everything we ought to have in a building and still keep the cost within reasonable bounds. We have all been pretty well agreed on most items, but on one we are hung up: the majority of our committee wants to include in our building budget enough money to pay for a number of works of art and ornamental pieces throughout the building. We don't think we are going overboard, but it would add between 1 and 2% to our total building costs; and our CEO is planting his feet against it. I don't think he is so much opposed to it himself as he is afraid that his board of directors and finance committee will criticize him. We feel our program is not an extravagance, but a good investment in employee morale and in community relations. If you agree, can you add anything that will bolster our case with the boss and his directors?

A In principle I agree—although so much depends on how you do it. You could spend your entire budget on one painting or sculpture and accomplish nothing except a few "Gee whiz" exclamations and a greater number of grumbles: "Why did they squander all that money showing off that way? They could have raised our salaries," or "lowered prices," or "helped our Little League team." But I gather from your letter that you are thinking of a building-wide program, and that is good.

The time is past when employers should feel any need to apologize for introducing beauty into a work environment or to think of it as an extravagance. The late Dr. Abraham Maslow, in his studies of people's basic needs, showed that the need for beauty was deep-seated, that ugliness could actually be sickening to many individuals. His experiments showed that the effects of ugliness were universally dulling and stultifying, that in strictly biological terms one needs beauty as one needs minerals in the diet.

Part of that can be accomplished without spending extra money—just by using imagination and taste, as Richard Gump, the San Francisco art dealer, wrote in his book *Good Taste Costs No More*. The judicious use of color can convert corridors, for example, from drab tunnels to cheerful walkways. In the work space itself there are even more options. A big room with dozens of clerical workers can either be an institutional barracks where all personal identity is sunk into the monotony of the surroundings, or be turned into a bright, stimulating setting just by the choice of color and textures in walls, furniture, and floor and window coverings, combined with thoughtful grouping of the furniture and equipment.

Your concern for community relations has more to do with the outside of the building than the inside. Modern-day high-rise construction, with its glass-box sameness and almost total lack of ornamentation, is not a very exciting addition to a community unless it is relieved by something beyond the structure. Most buildings—and most communities—are enhanced by landscaping; and if you are thinking of something sculptured, a landscaped setting is often the most effective.

But let me warn you: when you use landscaping, you are committing yourselves to a maintenance cost forever. You cannot have a tree, a shrub, a lawn, or a flower bed without taking care of it; and you would be better never to have any of these than to plant them and then neglect them. Nothing looks shabbier.

The same thing is true with any greenery you use inside: planters to divide space, plants to decorate offices or work areas. They must be attended, and occasionally replaced.

This is not to discourage you—I hope you do it—but to make you realistic. A commitment to landscape maintenance is equivalent to a capital investment, and you must decide how far you are prepared to go.

Your estimate of 1 to 2% added to your building cost is not far out of line: 1% of construction cost for works of art is a rule of thumb in government buildings, and some companies have spent more than that. But remember that within your basic construction budget probably 10% or more will be spent on the interior and as much on the exterior for items that are essentially aesthetic, and all subject to your discretion: paint, floor coverings, wall coverings, window coverings, even the exterior "skin" of your building, not to speak of furniture and fixtures of all kinds. Every item gives you another chance to add beauty, warmth, and cheer to your environment, and in most cases at no extra cost.

After you have examined all those options and made sure that you are getting your maximum aesthetic dollar's worth out of the 20% you would be spending anyway, you will be in much better shape to spend that extra 1 or 2% wisely and sensitively. You will know better which areas need that little extra lift and focus of interest that knowledgeably placed art will supply.

Making Choices
for the Work Environment

Q I hear what you say about the use of art and color to add beauty inside and outside of a company building, but who is going to choose the art and make the decisions on color and materials? I don't feel that I am knowledgeable enough to trust my own judgment.

A You have just made the first step in wisdom when you say you don't trust your own judgment alone. This is one of the few areas (personnel selection being the principal other one) where opinions and judgments should be shared even if one persom must make the final decision. Even more than in selecting people, personal taste and bias are bound to be involved in matters of art. Taste is highly subjective, and there are few if any absolutes. There are, however, a few guidelines and warning signals that your selection team can profitably heed.

Before you settle on *who* should manage, make a few guideline decisions of your own. They will help you in taking the next step. Here are a few for you to consider:

1. You are exposing this art and aesthetic treatment to people with a wide range of backgrounds, sophistication, and taste. Even though it may seem to be watering down the quality of your end result, you should avoid going too far out toward the special preferences or enthusiasms of any segment of your "public."

2. Whatever you buy is going to be around for a long time, so don't go in for fads; stay with what has stood the test of at least a generation of time.

3. If you want to display—and encourage—the more experimental, do it by setting aside space in a lobby or other area that is easily accessible to the public, and permit rotating exhibitions.

4. If your company is international, art—or historic artifacts—from the countries where you operate can add extra interest; and even in your permanent collection it can allow you more artistic latitude just because of what it is.

5. If you do invite the showing of outside works, be sure to set up procedures beforehand—criteria for selecting or rejecting, understanding as to security and other liability.

As to who should do your selecting, the one thing I would not do is to turn it over entirely to anyone outside your company. The danger is that such a person will have a field day indulging his or her own taste without regard to your needs.

Consult all you please; in fact, your selectors should do a lot of consulting with competent advisers, especially on what is available, where, and at what prices. Depending on how much expertise is available "in-house," you may need to include in your budget some provision for retaining some such counselors; but don't let them make final decisions—keep those in the hands of your own people. Your consultants should tell you what they like or don't like about particular selections or approaches. Then if you have to be referee to break deadlocks, you will have more basis for your judgment.

For your art-selection task force, look around your company to see if you can identify three or four people who have some personal history of involvement with or appreciation of art and aesthetics. If you have been in their homes, recall what they have done there—or in their offices—to see if you would trust their judgment on a broader scale.

Recognizing that most executives' homes—and many of their offices—are decorated by their wives, don't overlook this source of guidance. There are always potential problems, of course, when you involve wives in company business; but if you enlist the others first and then consult them as to their willingness to have a wife join them as an adviser, you should avoid problems.

You are not likely to make your building a great museum of art when your decisions are filtered through such a process. But that is not—and should not be—your goal.

How to Push for New Ideas

Q I have a good team of executives in my top management group except for one thing: none of them seems very creative or innovative. We need more new ideas than we are getting, if we want to stay competitive and to grow. Do we have to go out and hire special people just for that, or retain creative consultants, or is there some other way to lick the problem?

A Short range, if you have a problem with a specific product or product line, you might have to look outside for such things as design talent, possibly by contract. But if you are thinking long range, there are many other things you should look at first.

The creative ideas seldom come from the people at the top—not because they don't have imagination, but because, typically, they let themselves get so weighed down by their managing chores that they don't have (or don't *take*) time to let the creative hemisphere of their brains work. So the real push comes from the younger people, the hungry ones who are trying to make their way to the top. But it becomes a forward thrust only if the people at the top are receptive to it—if they maintain a climate where creative ideas are welcomed and pushed.

So that is the role of top man: to make sure that innovative ideas—and people—are encouraged.

While you should be alert to obviously creative people when you are hiring and recruiting, don't forget that everyone of average intelligence has some degree of creativity if it can be released and developed. Everyone can generate some ideas. It is not easy to bring out the creativity in people who have not been in the habit of expressing it. But it is very simple and easy to destroy it: it can be done with a word, or a look.

The real enemy of creativity in a working group is The Sneer. It can be spoken or unspoken. I had a boss who could kill an idea faster by just wrinkling his nose, as if he smelled a bad odor, than most people could with a five-minute speech.

So what you have to work toward is an environment, an atmosphere, in which people can offer new ideas without being slapped down. Not every idea has to be accepted; but each idea should be treated with respect. If the common response to a new suggestion is "Aw hell, we've tried that before," or "That couldn't possibly work"—especially if the tone of the words carries an implication that the suggester must be a little nuts or he wouldn't have brought it up—ideas can dry up like a Dust Bowl.

Building the right climate has to start with you—first with the example you set. If you are one who sneers and belittles, the people around will be quick to pick that up and reflect it all the way down the line. But if you show that you appreciate innovative ideas, even when you cannot accept and adopt all of them, that too can be contagious.

But you will need to go beyond your own example, by getting the word firmly to your top team, and from them down through the next levels, that this is the atmosphere you want to create and maintain.

One place to watch closely, if you don't want ideas killed, is in your bureaucracy. Midway down, somewhere in the bowels of the castle, there is always someone and often a network of supervisors who don't want the boat rocked by new ideas. You may have to deal with them in a variety of ways—first, trying to reverse their pattern by rewarding those who have helped to encourage innovation by others (the message will soon get around), and at the same time setting up a suggestion system that permits bypassing the bureaucratic roadblock. That too must be administered by open-minded people; but there is plenty of precedent and experience with suggestion systems to guide you.

One reason why people should not be discouraged from surfacing ideas is that even the most zany, unworkable idea may trigger a good one in someone else's mind. That has been demonstrated in the brainstorming exercises that have been so popular in some companies.

While I am not enthusiastic about brainstorming as a part of the mainstream operating process, it is an excellent way to loosen and open up the creative processes of people who have not used that part of their brains.

One word of caution if you wake up to discover that you have hired, or uncovered, a one-man idea factory. You will have problems of a different sort: such a person can be very hard to handle, but don't let it throw you, or discourage you from welcoming creativity.

The typical problem with such a person is not that his ideas are no good, but that he scatters himself in all directions; and that if these ideas are in his own field for execution, he never follows through but shoots off in another direction before he has completed the first one. You will have to decide where his greatest strengths lie, and whether you can keep him channeled in that direction. Don't give up lightly on him.

Creativity—and the People at the Top

In the preceding chapter I responded to a reader who was concerned about the lack of creativity and innovation among those in the top management of his company.

I replied that the top was not the place to look for creativity; that the real creative push is more likely to come from the younger people, the hungry ones who are trying to make their way to the top; but that this becomes a forward thrust only if the people at the top are receptive to it—if they maintain a climate where creative ideas are welcomed and pushed.

Now comes another reader who asks for some specifics about what the people at the top can do. He also adds one new dimension to what I had written: he wants to know if "the people at the top" include the board of directors.

The experience of a company whose whole corporate history has been one of innovation offers some answers to both questions. Dr. Bernard M. Oliver, who is vice president for research and development of Hewlett-Packard, recently discussed these and other related aspects of creativity.

Dr. Oliver agrees that the people at the top—and he includes the board of directors—have a key role to play if the company is to have effectively innovative people. He stresses again that the innovation itself does not come from boards of directions or CEOs, but that there are specific things these upper-echelon people can do to keep the creative juices flowing.

One major difference between Dr. Oliver's operation and that of my earlier reader is that Hewlett-Packard has formally organized research and development, while the earlier company did not. But even the word "formally" might be challenged: when people ask Dr. Oliver how he manages R & D at his company, he tells them, "I don't manage it—I provide an environment in which people can be creative. That consists of furnishing the tools they need. That consists of sympathetically listening, evaluating and ranking the projects they propose. And it consists of giving them a good deal of freedom for an early investigation of the viability of those projects."

In two respects, this company differs even from many of the other companies that invest heavily in R & D. For one thing, the management has found it more successful to have a single development team in the company carry an invention or product through from its inception to its marketing. As Dr. Oliver says, "We do not have one laboratory labeled 'R & D,' one labeled 'Production Engineering' and another labeled 'Production,' in which the product is tossed over the fence to somebody's doorstep, there possibly to die. We have removed those fences. One team has the responsibility for carrying its particular projects through to commercial success."

The other difference is in the involvement of everybody up to and including the board of directors. As Dr. Oliver says, "Now what can the boards of directors do? They cannot innovate. Generally they are too old and do not know what the problems are. But they ask questions of the management and make sure that there is an innovative team on board. We regularly expose our board of directors to our R and D program. After our board of directors meeting, we have a show-and-tell. One department or another will come in to show some of the newest and most exciting products and we explain the program.

"This is a great moment for these young people who have been with the company eight or ten years. Suddenly they are asked to give a presentation before the board of directors of Hewlett-Packard, a 2.4-billion-dollar company. Suddenly there is a link between them and the top. And they like it. They give good presentations. There is a lot of enthusiasm. And a lot of good questions are asked by the board. That keeps the board apprised of the things that all of us are doing."

Creativity by Seminar

Q We have been solicited several times by people who conduct seminars on creativity. Some of them have invited us to send one or more of our people to a seminar somewhere else, where they would join with people from other companies. The others have wanted to come into our own headquarters and put on a seminar just for our own people.

Aside from the fact that these programs are not cheap, our people would be taken away from their jobs for anywhere from one to several days. Do you think these programs are worth the price in dollars and time?

A There is nothing wrong with the *general* idea; anything that stimulates creativity and innovation can be valuable. But there are many *particulars* to be looked at.

For one, there are degrees of skill and effectiveness among the many practitioners who have entered this field. If you decide to try it, you should do some screening before you sign up with anyone. You are entitled to know all about the background and credentials of the person or persons who would be conducting your seminar. You should also know about their track record: what do their previous clients have to say (to you, not to the seminar producer) about the results and worthwhileness of the program?

There is another step that comes ahead of that, though: there is no use sending people to creativity seminars if the climate around your company is not hospitable to new ideas. Don't send anyone whose boss is an idea killer—or anyone who must submit ideas to a committee whose chairman or members are idea assassins.

I once saw a list of "22 Ways to Kill an Idea." Without trying to recite all twenty-two, I can recap them—at least the deadliest and most common ones—into a few lethal categories. The Sneer. The Shrug. The Lifted Eyebrow. The Deadly Silence. The Referral to a Committee. Accompanying any of these (any but Deadly Silence) are such encouraging comments as "You aren't really serious about that, are you?" or "We've tried that many times before and its utterly impracticable" or its opposite, "It's never been tried"—implying that obviously if it had any merit, somebody would have thought of it before. Mention of how much it would cost to put the idea into operation will smother any consideration of the savings it might bring.

If you have people in your company who practice such lethal tactics (and what company doesn't have a few?), they are the first ones you should send to the creativity seminar. If by chance you are one of the culprits (probably not, or you wouldn't have raised the question—but look at yourself as squarely as you can), maybe you should lead the way.

Once your corporate environment—under your leadership and example—has been made receptive instead of hostile to the flow of innovative ideas, you won't have to search very far to find them. They are all around you, if you open up to them.

As I said earlier, I don't usually expect to find the most creative ideas among senior management people: they are so busy making decisions on what is right in front of them that they don't take time to generate the innovative ideas, and most of the creative push comes from the hungry young people who are trying to make their way to the top. These young people haven't yet learned what can't be done. Many of their ideas, consequently, *will* be impracticable and will have to be patiently screened out. But you don't need a very large ratio of good ones if you have a good total supply coming in.

So the role of the top man—and it applies to the top of the branch office and the top of the department just as it does to the top of the organization—is to make sure that he has guys around him who are full of bright ideas—and that they stay that way by being encouraged and welcomed.

If a seminar is useful, in your circumstances, in getting the process kicked off, it may be worth the price in time and money. But the other factors come first.

X

The Board of Directors: Friend or Foe?

Employees are not the only people with whom an executive must deal. In today's world, being an executive has become more and more of a "relations" job. The number of the relationships, with both public and private groups, has increased at the same time that the potential impact of each of them has magnified.

Some of these relations the chief executive can delegate, but some he cannot. When a company's shares are publicly owned, he has a responsibility to the board of directors that is all his; and to governmental agencies there is an accountability that is ultimately his even though others may handle the details.

His grasp of these relationships—how he perceives them and how he conducts them—is another test of his stature as an executive.

213

"Meddling" Directors

Q Last year I took my company public. The stock underwriters insisted that we enlarge the board of directors and bring in a majority of outside directors. Now, these new directors are poking their noses into every corner of our business. They ask questions about all kinds of things that I don't think are any of their business. They want to know all of our costs and expenditures, the relative profitablity of different product lines, everybody's salary and our compensation practices. They are even beginning to tell us what all our ratios should be: debt to equity, return on investment, gross and net profit margins, etc.

I know all these things are important, but I think I know as much as they do about what's right for our business. It is a real pain in the neck to have to explain or justify everything I do to these outsiders. I wonder if I am going to be able to run my business if they are going to dip into every area of my operations. If other companies have this kind of meddling, how do their chief executives stand it?

A What you—and every founder-operator—have to recognize is that when you "go public," you *are* public. To get the public's money, you gave up a lot of private freedom.

Check yourself every time you say "my company." You sold your company when you went public. You may be the largest shareholder, but you are now an employee—in a company that is publicly owned. The sooner you understand your new job, the more effective you'll be.

Those outside directors who are being such a nuisance were put on your board for a reason. They are there to represent all the shareholders, not just the new ones, in seeing that the company is being properly managed. That means they *have* to monitor the performance of management—you.

And they must oversee all the use and disposition of every company asset. They are there to be busybodies.

If you get into a financial bind because you have not maintained the right kind of capital structure or have not managed your cash prudently, you are not the only one who will be held responsible; disgruntled shareholders will look to the directors as much as to you for damages if they can prove bad management.

Today's legal environment puts any corporate director in jeopardy. He or she is vulnerable to shareholder, employee, consumer, and other class-action or derivative lawsuits. But such liability is only one of the legal land-mines. Direct punitive action under statutes and regulations growing out of such legislation as ERISA (the law governing private pension), for instance, poses another exposure, one that's more hazardous each year.

Only a highly imprudent person would accept a directorship if he or she could not feel free—and competent—to get reliable answers to all the kinds of questions you mention, plus some you haven't thought of yet.

Indeed these quantitative, dollars-and-cents kinds of questions may be the easiest for the directors to ask and for you to answer. This is particularly true now that directors are increasingly expected to represent more than just the interests of the shareholders. Believe it or not, they are expected to represent the public interest more broadly, and to monitor the company's performance in social areas as well as economic and financial.

This rapid expansion of the law has led to the creation (legally required in many situations) of audit committees, and of social-policy, conflict-of-interest, and various other board-level committees. All such changes increase the independence of outside directors by requiring them to monitor new aspects of the company. This trend has also led to pressures to define more narrowly who is an outsider on the board. An outsider truly has to be at arm's length.

So, it could be that "you ain't seen nothin' yet."

But having recited all these sources of possible tension between you and your board, let me remind you that there is another side to the coin: you and the board should want the same thing—the most profitable, successful operation the company could possibly have. Once you look upon them as helpers more than meddlers, the whole climate may change.

So lift that big chip off your shoulder and look at what the directors, individually and as a group, can do for you. It is just barely possible that you don't know everything there is to know about marketing, capital structure, public offerings of securities, salary administration, pension administration, and the host of other problems superimposed on the nuts-and-bolts part of your management job.

Your directors may not have all the answers, either; but collectively they have, or have access to, a greater pool of knowledge than you can have all by yourself. If not, you picked the wrong directors.

Treat them as a built-in kind of consulting service. You're still CEO, and you haven't given up your autonomy in what is truly management's area. The line between what is policy and what is management may seem hazy to one who has been in full charge on both sides of the line. But that line is clear and can be drawn so that both sides respect it.

P.S. If you are still fussing about those nosy members of your board of directors, remember that your directors will be less inclined to inject themselves into your purely management bailiwick if you do not arouse their hostility—and their suspicions—by trying to keep them from exercising their proper role as directors. Like the apple of knowledge in the Garden of Eden, there's nothing anybody wants so much as information you try to deny them.

Going Public

Q My company is privately owned; my wife and I and members of our immediate family own the majority of the stock, and a few close friends own the rest.

We have been growing so fast that we need more capital. Some of our minority owners have been telling me that we should go public to raise the extra capital. They argue that having publicly traded stock would make it easier from then on to sell shares whenever we had to increase our capital, as we probably will have to do from time to time. They also say it will make it easier to borrow from banks.

This all may be true, but I don't feel comfortable about selling stock to a lot of outsiders. Am I wrong?

A You are not wrong to be concerned, and to think carefully about all the alternatives before you jump at any of them. What your co-owners tell you is true—with a few qualifications: Being publicly traded does not automatically create a dependable market for a stock; someone in the investment fraternity usually has to cooperate in "making a market." But the public offering is the first step.

As for borrowing from banks, having public stock is not usually a major factor in itself; but it does have some indirect effects that are helpful in certain special circumstances. Banks like to lend money to companies where they know and have confidence in management and in the future of the operation. When there are doubts, the kinds of disclosure required of public companies give the lender some further insight; and the existence of a public market in the stock adds some flexibility and a degree of confirmation of valuations.

But the very things that help the lender also impose some additional burden on the company: the moment a company's stock is publicly offered and traded, the company becomes subject to requirements of filing reports, to SEC for example, that were never required before and can become very burdensome.

When your minority-owning friends recommend going public, they may be thinking about their own estate problem even more than the company's capital needs. Many a company has made its first public stock offering—or offer to sell the whole company—because the founder and original investors had their nest egg all tied up in unmarketable stock. Secondary offerings of part of their holdings, accompanying the company's primary offering, have helped to "tidy up" their estates by providing cash for eventual estate taxes.

You should weigh that same option into your own estate calculations.

But along with everything else you must decide what kind of company you want to have and what kind of place you want to have in it. You started your letter by saying "my company." The minute you go public it is no longer *your* company (even to the degree it now is, when you have relatives and friends involved with you). When you go public you *are* public. You not only will have other owners who will have rights to make demands on you, but you, and they, will have increased the leverage of your other partner—government.

Your other family members and your other investors will each have different motives in this decision, but to the extent that you are in control you will have to ask yourself at least these questions: "Which is more important to me—to have the company grow or for me to remain in control even if it doesn't grow? Does my temperament place more value on my independence or on the probable higher dollar rewards in selling out some of the independence? Am I willing to risk "hocking the family jewels" (putting up every cent I have or can borrow—and persuading my present fellow investors to do likewise) to supply more capital ourselves now, instead of inviting in the public, and hoping we can generate more capital internally before we have to face this alternative again? If we remain private, can I see orderly succession in the company after I am gone, when the surviving family members and other investors may all have different and conflicting ideas of how the company should be managed?"

The problem of succession does not hinge entirely on whether stock ownership is private or public; but there is a universal tendency for founder-operators under private control to act as if they were immortal and to postpone making any provision for orderly transition. Being publicly traded imposes not only the legal sanctions of SEC et al. but also the disciplines of the investment market itself to prod management into many moves that would otherwise stay forever on the back burner.

Use Your Directors

Q You have talked about the powers and duties of a board of directors. But ours is a closely held company and I can replace the whole board any time I want to. What use is a board like that?

A Only as much use as you are wise enough to make of them.

I won't go into the legal question whether you really can "hire and fire" directors at your whim; I'll let your legal staff settle that. But if you select your directors carefully, you can have a built-in consulting service that you could not afford to hire. It isn't always easy to attract good directors to a company like yours, or to any company today; but you will do better if they know that you are not looking for rubber stamps.

Since you can't possibly know everything there is to know about every phase of a business (if you think you do, you are thinking in very small dimensions), you should deliberately try to find people, not in the fields you know best, but in the ones you know least. But even more than technical know-how in a single field, you should look for broad corporate knowledge and judgment. Those qualities can help you find your way through a lot of present pitfalls in a fast-changing world; but they can also help with something you may not want to face: planning for your own ultimate succession.

Serving on Another Company's Board

Q I never have served on the board of directors of any company but my own; but I have just been invited to go on an outside board in a different industry. Is it wise to do it? I hear a lot of debate about corporate board service and read of the controversial proposals of SEC and Congress to change the composition and function of boards. So I wonder what I'm getting into.

A The more this debate rages, the more important it is that good sense prevail and no one be stampeded.

I happen to favor the trend toward outsider-dominated boards; I think it is as good for the company involved as for the public interest. But it will be good only to the extent that the outside directors are of good quality.

Some critics and observers are insisting that no chief executive should serve on any corporate board except his own. This view, I feel, is very shortsighted and not in the public interest. If every corporation adopted this rule (or had it imposed upon it by law or regulation), then no corporation would be able to look to this pool of corporate management talent for potential directors; and there would not be enough others in all of America with enough business and corporate experience, knowledge, and judgment to provide the policy guidance that would be needed by all the corporations in the country.

You must balance that against your obligation to your own company—plus the hazards to you in today's legal climate.

Your company and you can benefit from the experience if the other company is substantial and the other directors are people of broad experience. The broader business outlook, the interchange, and the insight into how other enterprises handle business and public problems are the major remaining reasons why executives accept outside directorships; the prestige of being on a prominent board and associating with prominent people has lost some of its shine in recent years as the burdens and hazards have grown.

And there are real burdens and hazards. If you do go on this board, be sure you get all the protection that is available from directors' liability insurance and indemnification resolutions; but since even those cannot give you full protection, be prepared to spend a lot of hours on homework. You must keep yourself informed so that your votes can be those of a prudent director.

You say that this board is in another industry; even so, check for possible conflict of interest, which can rise up to cause you problems.

Aside from these potential hazards, your biggest problem is to be sure that the time and attention required by this board service do not interfere with your performance in your own job. This is not materially different from the time problem every

businessman must handle whenever he works on anything
other than his own job; and in today's world the effective executive *must* spend time and effort on other matters than the
immediate job of running his own company. It has long been accepted doctrine that an executive could not spend 100% of his
time on his company management job; the figure of 20% used
to be most often mentioned as the proper portion to allocate to
outside affairs—community work, industry association efforts,
governmental affairs, and public relations generally. That 20%
figure has been creeping up and up.

This has led some companies—and their advisers—to propose
that the top command of the company be divided between a
Mr. Inside and a Mr. Outside. (I do not favor this proposal.)

It is in this context that service on other company's boards
must be viewed. Anyone who is fit for a major job in a company
must be able to manage his own time and to set priorities. He
must be responsible enough to know how much time he needs
to get the results he is after in his own job. Whether it be an
outside corporate board, a civic undertaking, or golf, if he
neglects his job to pursue the other interest, it will show up in
his performance. Ultimately he will face the consequences.

Any competent executive will sense when his time allocations
are getting out of balance, and will make his own adjustments
before anyone else has reason to criticize his performance.

In this perspective, I think that three outside directorships are
as many as any active corporate officer, including the chief
executive, should attempt to handle. Even three may be too
many at certain periods in the affairs of the corporate officer's
own or the other companies; but that is just another of the
many priority decisions he must make, as a matter of his own
prudence. I would not want to see any number specified as a
legal limit.

XI

The Other Relationships of the Executive

In addition to those places where the law prescribes the interface of the company—and hence of its executive—with public agencies and corporate entities, the public presents itself in an almost infinite number of forms and segments: community, consumer, environmental, religious and racial, special-interest and single-interest groups. Contact or communication with these groups is optional; but a company ignores their existence at its peril.

Sheer numbers would dictate that the executive could not maintain many, if any, of these contacts himself. Yet the quality and effectiveness of any contact that is established by others in his company will inescapably reflect his attitude toward such relationships.

Management's Flyspecking Ruins PR

Q I am not an executive, buy *my* survival is at stake, and I suspect there are dozens of others like me whose innards are being eaten out by the indignity and demeaning treatment they receive at the hands of a well-meaning but thoughtless boss. If you have a good answer, maybe you will publish it with my letter in the hope that my boss and others like him will see it.

As head of Corporate Communications (a fancy name for PR) I am responsible for writing and production of all news releases, of which we issue many; and for our annual report, which has to do many different jobs for our company all in one piece.

Now I know there are many correct ways to say the same thing; and I make no claim that my writing style is God's gift to journalism. But I am at least a good journeyman professional in my craft, and the one thing I do know better than anyone in our company is what the news media expect technically, in a release. In the annual report, it is my job to develop agreement early in the game as to what we want to accomplish by the report; and while others might write it just as well, one person has to make sure there is a consistent style, organization, and structure to accomplish what we're after.

But every time we are going to make anything but the most routine announcement, our president insists on going over the news release and doing his own editing of it. If he has any misgivings—which he usually does—he calls in two or three others (most often our general counsel, and maybe the controller or our economist) and lets them go over it. By the time they are through flyspecking it—not just for facts, but for grammar, punctuation, sentence structure, you name it—it is a mishmash. Then I am supposed to send it out to the papers over my name.

With the annual report it is the same thing, only they have more time to rework it page by page so that it comes out even more jumbled.

Not only am I judged professionally by the quality of what comes out of my shop, but I also am judged and rated internally by the results we get in the press, in the investment fraternity, and elsewhere from the releases and reports we issue. If the things we send out are considered amateurish and second-rate by the professionals who get them, we are going to get second-rate treatment; so both the company and I suffer. This is not just an assumption. It has already happened, and I have been given friendly warnings by people on the receiving end, in the media.

Am I right in thinking that the president and the others around him should keep their hands off this work that I am hired to handle?

A I don't want to promote mutiny or suggest that you quit your job. But I have to tell you (and your boss) that no self-respecting PR chief should put up with that nonsense for a minute.

Of course it is reasonable for sensitive releases—and certainly annual-report texts—to be reviewed by key members of management. But they are reviewed for fact and policy, not for style. If the others have corrections or suggestions, they should send those back to you and let you incorporate them into the text as you see fit. Writing is one thing that cannot be done by a committee.

Occasionally the "reviewers" may suggest changes in style, too—especially if they think your wording does not make the facts or policy clear enough. (In my experience, though, the management people and especially the lawyers are the ones who don't want things stated too clearly—they prefer to leave them fuzzy and weaselly.) In any case, you should be the final judge of release language and style; and in the long run, if management doesn't like your style, management is just going to have to get a new boy.

Which leads to the key point: I believe that any PR chief who is worth his salt must be willing to lay his job on the line every day of his life: to call things the way he sees them and to stand up to his boss for good professional handling of the company's representations and disclosures. I know that isn't the popular image of public relations, which many people dismiss as flackery; but it is the right professional view. One of the worst public relations gaffes in recent years resulted from a PR head not standing up to his boss on just such an issue. If your relations with your boss are not on that basis and you don't have the backbone to work toward putting them on that basis, not belligerently but maturely and firmly—there is no point in your fussing about the details. Reconcile yourself to the fact that you will always be miserable as long as you stay in that role.

P.S. What I say above about management kibitzers esmasculating public relations copy applies equally to advertising copy. In fact, the ones who dabble in one are likely to be the same ones who dip into the other. It is the old story of "too many cooks."

Management and the head of advertising should be in agreement about the general approach and tone of the advertising campaign; and then management must depend upon the advertising chief to deal with the agency. If management does not have confidence in the advertising manager, it should get a new manager. If together they do not have confidence in their agency, they should get a new one. But unless they want to waste a large part of their advertising budget, the rest of the management crew should keep their hands off.

Public Relations
and Advertising

Q I see that some of the biggest national public relations firms are being taken over by some of the major advertising agencies. The assumption seems to be that advertising and public relations are, as one of the firms put it, "complementary tools in the solution of modern communications problems," and that combining them will provide economies of scale.

Does that suggest that these same functions should be combined internally within a company—that our in-house advertising and public relations departments should be combined?

A Not if your conception of public relations is anything like mine.

If you are thinking only of getting your company's name in the paper, or even if you're thinking only of promoting the sale of your product, both of those are perfectly legitimate functions. But don't confuse them with public relations, in its most basic sense. Both of those are *publicity* activities. Publicity is used as one of the tools of public relations, but it also is used in marketing and sales, which have nothing to do with PR.

Many large retail stores have traditionally called their advertising department the "publicity department," thereby signaling that the purpose was to publicize the store's wares by every means possible: paid space in the advertising columns and free space in the other columns. I was about to say "in the news columns," but the sections of the newspaper where the stores and their suppliers aim much of their publicity—society and gossip columns, food and houseware pages—are not usually true news sections.

Public relations, as I use the term, and as it is viewed by the more substantial practitioners in the field, is aimed at maintaining the legitimacy of the company or the industry—perception by the public that the company or industry is operating in the public interest and is serving a societal need.

A generation ago, anyone using those words might have been written off as an academic theorist. Today they are part of the operating language of any wisely managed company.

The person who advises top management on the public implications of company policies and decisions must be independent and objective in his judgments. Whether he is an in-house PR director or an outside consultant, if he can be influenced by pressures from the advertising or marketing forces, he is worthless to management as a PR counselor. He should be broadgauged enough himself to recognize the impact that his recommendations might have on marketing considerations; but neither that awareness nor, above all, pressure from marketing people should be able to muzzle him and keep him from presenting his professional appraisal of PR consequences.

It is the job of management—the lonesome, agonizing job—to weigh all the marketing, legal, financial, public relations, and other arguments for or against a proposal, and to arrive at a company decision. But management is entitled, in that process, to have the honest, informed—and independent—judgments of each of the advising spokesmen.

If public relations is made subordinate to any other discipline in the company, or in the services advising the company, its independence, its credibility—and its value—will be lost. In today's turbulent world, management cannot afford that loss.

In the meanwhile, *publicity* has a perfectly proper place in the marketing mix. In many fields, product promotion through publicity is an integral part of every sales campaign—especially to introduce a new product or a new model, or even to initiate a new season. Carefully timed to coordinate with advertising and personal contracts, publicity is aimed not only at special feature pages of the daily press and news desks of press, TV, and radio but also at a wide range of trade magazines where product recognition is an important support to the sales effort.

But let's call this by its right name. It is product-promotion publicity. It is a valuable corporate tool. But it is not public relations.

Because this promotion activity, though, like all other sales and marketing efforts, can have public policy overtones, it is important that there be close coordination between marketing and public relations. It is that need for coordination that had led—mistakenly, in my judgment—to occasional moves to consolidate the two functions administratively. Much better that they remain separate, with a "dotted line" dual responsibility of the kind that has to operate all through complex companies. Public relations should have no voice in the purely sales thrust of any advertising or promotional copy, but should be the constant watchdog for any social or other public implications, not only in the copy but in other aspects of the product of its marketing.

That watchdog role (often called the "social conscience" function) is not pointed at marketing, sales, or advertising any more than at any part of a company's operation. It must apply all across the board. But that underlines the importance of its not being subordinate to any of the functions it might be reviewing.

How these relationships are structured varies from company to company, as indeed it must with the diversity of geographic, divisional, profit-center, and other decentralization. But most of the major companies of this country observe the spirit of the relationship I have been describing, however it is structured.

Meeting Deadlines

Q Ours is a small-to-medium-sized company in a high-technology field. Even though competition is fierce in our field, our product line seems to be recognized as superior to most of our competitors on most of our items, because our sales are growing and apparently our share of market as well.

Our customers seem satisfied with the performance of our products, their only complaint being that we have a tendency to miss target delivery dates.

In spite of our steady growth, our earnings as a percentage of sales do not compare well with those of our competitors. Can you suggest where we should look for "leaks"? We don't think we have much fat or extravagance anywhere—in our payroll, our plant and quarters, or anywhere in operations. What's wrong?

A Your letter gives one clue that I would certainly check out as a likely "cause and effect" culprit: your delays in delivery. Whether they account for your subpar earnings or not,

237

they can breed other troubles for you and should be corrected, and it would be a fair bet that they are depressing your earnings in a chain-reaction kind of way that can infect a whole organization like a contagious disease.

Tempo is hard to maintain anywhere; but high-technology industries have their own special vulnerabilities. For example, key people with scientific backgrounds take understandable pride in perfection. Their preoccupation with checking and double-checking often gets in the way of deadlines.

Whether this or some other factor causes a deadline to be missed, once it is missed in one part of the operation the whole time schedule is thrown off. An organization, like a heart, is in trouble when it loses the normal rhythm of its work.

Perhaps you have not done all you could to help your people—all down the line in every department—to understand two things: the dollar value of timing, and the intricate interdependence that makes it possible for any one person in the company to throw that timing out of whack.

For example, if the standard lead time between booking an order and delivering the product (thus recording a completed sale) is twelve months, then accelerating the delivery by one month can make a difference of $8\frac{1}{3}\%$ in the annual reported earnings on that product.

The same rationale applies to other phases of the company operation: if a new building or a new machine is going to effect great savings in operating costs, then every day gained or lost in getting that building or that machine into operation simply hastens or postpones the plus effect of those savings in the earnings of the company.

Unless this is strongly, clearly hammered home—and by the boss himself—then there will be people who drag their feet, often convinced that they are serving the company well by doing it.

I have known company controllers and their lieutenants who would take great pride in delaying an authorized expenditure—the purchase of equipment, the hiring of people, or whatever. Acutely conscious of cash flow, they would reason that they had saved the company money by every month they could postpone that spending. They did not appreciate that unless the expenditure was going to make money for the company, it never should have been authorized in the first place; and if it was going to increase profits, then every day it was delayed simply postponed the beneficial effect on the company's earnings.

It is safe to state as a general principle that in any given state of the art, and at any given share of the market, the profits of the company will be measured not by the level of the technology, but by the performance of the entire corps of people—technical and nontechnical—in delivering that technology to the customer.

Employees often think we are dishing out platitudes (they have earthier words to describe them) when we tell them how important each individual is to the company's success. But in this matter of tempo and momentum, this is not platitude and no exaggeration. It's as real as the timing of a block in a football play. If one person is one day late in completing a subassembly, it doesn't at the most just delay the whole product by one day: by causing another assembling group to rearrange its schedules, it can start a succession of delays that can build up cumulatively to a week or weeks.

Once you have made the importance of timing clear all the way down the line, check on your production scheduling—your critical-path-method projections and all other elements of your planning. Be sure you have the participation and the commitment of the key people who will be responsible for seeing that each deadline is met: not only production deadlines, but the supply, paperwork, and endless other kinds of deadlines that can make or break the big deadline.

Once you lick your habit of delayed deliveries, you can expect several kinds of dividends:

First, you should get the direct, immediate effect of having earnings pushed forward into the current quarter and the current year, instead of their slopping over to later periods.

Second, you will be surer of keeping the customers happier, and thus breeding repeat orders.

Third, the biggest payoff may be more subtle: the healthier morale and esprit de corps that come from feeling pride in performance can bring better performance all through your company.

"Path" to Success

Q We manufacture large industrial-process machinery and equipment. Much of it is custom-designed, and some is standard; but most of it is sold under contracts with lead times of a year or more.

We do a pretty good job of estimating most of our costs, unit by unit, and yet our profit margins on the whole job end up smaller than they should be. Part of the reason involves inventory: we stock up too much, too soon, and have the extra cost of carrying it.

The other reason is related but different. The production crews working on one subassembly don't finish their portion by the time another crew needs it, so we have a double kind of extra cost: the second crew is marking time but can't be moved to another job, and meanwhile we have a "semifinished goods inventory" investment in the parts that crew has finished.

Do you have any remedy to suggest?

A You are right that the two problems are related—more related then different. Both involve scheduling, and that in turn involves everyone who works on the contract.

At the beginning of World War II the companies that were suddenly plunged into building ships and tanks and LSTs and other strange pieces of equipment they had never made before found themselves in some horrendous snafus of the kind you are describing. We might never have won the war if they had not licked the problem; and the techniques they developed then have gone on being refined for application to civilian industries.

Whole new professional disciplines, such as operations research, have grown up to deal with such problems as this, and whole new vocabularies have grown up to match. But the basics are really quite simple; and they have a parallel in one of the oldest of household arts, the preparation of a meal.

If your wife is a good cook and hostess who can deliver a several-course dinner on time and without great commotion, compare her with an inexperienced young bride putting on her first dinner party. The eager young thing plans a menu with all kinds of goodies that she knows her guests will like. But when the time arrives when they should be eating, the dinner is a disaster.

She has started everything cooking at the same time; her roast isn't half cooked yet, but her peas are cooked to death; her originally crisp salad is now wilted and soggy; a soufflé she had planned for dessert has risen like a sunburst, then fallen like a piece of shoe leather.

The only thing that even partially rescues her is that her guests have gone on drinking so many cocktails while waiting for the overdue dinner that by the time they sit down to eat they wouldn't know a vol-au-vent from a coq au vin.

Your wife, on the other hand, knows that these things have to be planned ahead and their timing coordinated. She probably never heard of the term, but she practices what has come to be known as the "critical path method" (CPM)—and that is what you should install in your plant (or plants: it sounds as though several plants may be involved in supplying your subassemblies).

Many excellent books have been written on the theory and practice of the CPM. But the essence of it, for your purpose, is this: The project manager on each contract, with the cooperation of the heads of each of the subassembly units, should put together the following time projections: How long will it take to complete each subassembly? At what point in each of those jobs will another subassembly need to be available for assembling with this one into an intermediate assembly? What critical items will need to be supplied by other suppliers, and at what point in this sequence? What quantities of what standard materials (steel plate, copper wire, etc.) will be needed, and on what timetable?

When all these separate determinations have been made, they can all be put together to see how they fit. Typically, they will be laid out on a bar chart with a bar for each component (in your case each subassembly) spanning the months (specific calendar months of a specific year). The bars will be broken into segments to represent the time to be spent (and the exact date involved) on each phase of each of the components: design, purchasing (order dates and delivery dates) manufacturing of component parts, assembling of parts, assembling with other subassembilies, final completion and delivery.

It is when these bar charts are laid out one above the other that the whole thing comes clearly into focus.

If you want to read a little more about this process, there is a good treatment of it in Charles C. Martin's book *Project Man-*

agement—How to Make It Work, published by the American Management Association. For a much longer treatment, but with some good charts and graphs to illustrate exactly how to go about it, McGraw-Hill published in 1965 a book called *The Critical Path Method,* by Shaffer, Ritter, and Meyer.

A newer and more sophisticated approach called material requirements planning (MRP) is being widely adopted by American industry. But it is designed for manufacturing, whereas CPM is more appropriate to project undertakings; and I gather that your production has more of the characteristics of a project than of a manufacturing operation. To make MRP work for you, moreover, you have got to be prepared to go all the way in installing the support systems that have to go with it.

If you have never used any of these techniques, you will probably find your results greatly improved just by adopting the simpler, straightforward CPM concept. You should go further and get yourself familiar with the newer MRP systems; but I would advise you not to commit yourself and your operation to it until you are sure you know how much you are biting off.

Public Affairs

Q I am in a business that is very community-related, so that we are expected to play an active (often a leading) part in every community project and organization. More than that, many of the organizations insist on having only the top executive from each company on their boards. I am in sympathy with what these organizations (most of them!) are doing, but it takes more of my time than I really can spare. Is there any good answer?

A Your problem is not unique, and is not limited to your field. In almost every line of business that involves much direct public contact—with customers or with community affairs—the CEO is called upon to do more things, be in more places, serve on more boards and committees, make more speeches than any one human being could possibly do. The only way you can possibly keep your sanity and still run your business effectively is to devise some way of sorting out all these demands and putting priorities on them.

The first step in screening is to pass as many as possible on down to your subordinates—not just to relieve the pressure on you, but because the experience and the exposure will be good for them.

I know the organizations will at first resist your delegating these assignments; but just because they "insist" on you does not mean that you have to do what they insist. It still is your time and your decision.

But if you want to be most helpful to them, you will try to persuade them that they are missing the target. What they really want, of course, is not you, but what they think you and your name will bring to the organization. You can point out to them that they can get two (maybe three) for the price of one: that they will get the energy, enthusiasm—and greater time—of the younger executive; that he will have your backing on anything that really needs it; and (if it is true) that he is a comer who is slated for bigger things in the company. But after you have exhausted that process, there still may be more than you can handle, whose sponsors will not settle for anyone but you. At that point, apply my "five-year test" (see page 7), and since many of these dilemmas involve conflict with family priorities, use both parts of the test: in addition to asking yourself which way the company will be better off, also ask yourself, "Which way will my family be better off five years from now—if I do this or if I don't?"

You will be surprised how this test will put some things into different perspective, and help to sort out "the important from the urgent."

Who in Management
Should Handle
Public Affairs?

Q What you say about serving on community organization boards and committees makes a lot of sense, and I think I am taking care of that problem in just about the way you suggested. Af first I had a hard time selling the idea, but now it seems to be working well, both for the organizations and for us in the company.

But that is only part of the problem, for me and every other CEO I talk to. We are all having to spend time on another kind of "public affairs" we never thought of ten years ago: meeting and talking with government agency heads, legislators, regulators, trade associations, and all manner of "public interest" groups that have involved themselves in public action on issues affecting our businesses.

These public activities are taking so much of my time that I do not have enough time left for running my business. I know I have to make some changes, and probably do some reorganization of our top command. The question is *what* changes and *what* reorganization? Everybody insists only the top man can

247

handle these public negotiations, because he must be able to make decisions and commit the company. Some say that I should devote full time to these activities, as "Mr. Outside," and let a "Mr. Inside" run the company.

I have so many personal misgivings about that kind of move that I'm not sure I am thinking straight about it. What do you think: is this the way to go, or is there a better way?

A You are not alone in any part of your problem—either the time burden or your bewilderment as to how to handle it.

What used to be largely a big-business concern (and not such an all-absorbing problem for top management there) is now plaguing managements of medium-sized and even fairly small companies.

A few years ago we began to hear moaning that top executives were spending as much time on public affairs as on running the business itself. Today it is even worse.

During all the years I was growing up in business a common rule of thumb for good allocation of time was 80% for strictly company affairs, and 20% for all outside activities. Today the facts are nearly reversed for many executives—they find only 20 to 25% of their time available for their jobs (at least for their jobs as they have traditionally been specified: the job specs may need to be revised to recognize more of this area as a regular part of the job.)

As a solution, I do not think this "Mr. Outside–Mr. Inside" approach is the right answer. If it is true—and I think it is—that the official who represents the company in these public-affairs sessions must be able to speak for the company—be able to make decisions, to commit—then Mr. Outside would soon begin to disqualify himself. If he is spending 100% of his time on public affairs, he will be too remote from the company's decision-making processes to be able to make wise decisions and commitments himself.

Even before this current surge of public-affairs pressures, I never have favored the practice of designating one person to spend full time on community and public-service activities. The theory is that it relieves the regular operating people of the burden of the public activities; but in practice, the full-time professional public servant soon comes to be known as a person without authority in the company.

Much better that the company be represented in all these assignments by people who have basic operating responsibilities; and that the burden be shared as widely as will still be effective.

For the most sensitive of the relationships—particularly those involving government policy—the assignment could not be shared by more than a handful of the most senior officers. To make it work properly even for them, though, calls for some reassessment and redefinition of responsibilities. It involves practicing the best of the art of being an executive.

First, the CEO and his senior associates should have the best of staff work, for both their internal and their external sessions. They should not have to use up their time gathering data, or plowing through inadequately organized and summarized material. The staff should bring issues to them well crystallized.

The CEO—and his senior team likewise—must push downstream many higher-level decisions than we would have thought proper a decade ago. Capital expenditures, for example—even product decisions that don't change the whole direction of the company—that once would have required top management approval may now have to be "reported" instead.

The CEO will have to be tougher than ever in his picking and choosing which meetings, appearances, negotiations *only* he can cover. This should always have been part of his priority process; but now he has a new dimension to add to his criteria.

It is always a judgment call—but there is a fine line beyond which he can be *too* visible.

Square Pegs
and Square Holes

Q You have advised against the "Mr. Outside–Mr. Inside" approach to public affairs and implied that this should be part of the duties of all the senior officers of a company.

But aren't some executives better suited to this kind of activity than others? Isn't it a waste of the time and talents of those who are not cut out for it, to involve them in these public dealings? Wouldn't it be better to concentrate those in the hands of someone with special aptitude for it?

A It might be, if there were not other considerations that far outweigh that one.

Two factors in particular are germane to your question:

The first is that these "outside" pressures and demands on executive time are not just little minor nuisances. Annoying and distracting as they might be to someone who would rather be working on next year's model or the next corporate acquisition, these pressures are not little mosquitoes that would disappear if we just had the right kind of spray gun.

251

They are a built-in, integral part of the corporate environment. Business has always existed by public franchise (today we say it has to prove its "legitimacy"). Every business operates in a goldfish bowl of public visibility and scrutiny.

But that is only part of the story. The very success of our enterprising business ingenuity, coupled with our amazing technology, has projected the business machinery into every part of the world and into every walk of life in our own country. The result is an interdependence, between countries and between all segments of society, that would be as hard to reverse as to unscramble an omelet.

So everything business does cuts across some part of the concerns of every agency of government and of voluntary civic groups that concern themselves with the "public interest."

But the result of having to deal with all those public pressures is not all bad. It may seem to be totally restrictive: narrowing the bounds of what business is *allowed* to do. But to the alert, perceptive executive, these sessions and contacts may also reveal new areas of opportunity.

Certainly the future course and shape of business are going to be affected by the total impact of all these public confrontations.

So the decision makers of business, who have to map out the future course of their own enterprise, need to have some direct contact with and some personal feel for these public forces that may influence that course.

The second factor that bears on your question is one that is only beginning to be realized: that chief executives hereafter will be expected to include among their qualifications all the skills and qualities that are required for effectiveness in the public-affairs area. They must not only be articulate and capable in their interpersonal dealings, but they must also have the sensitivity and the intellectual breadth to recognize and understand the conflicting attitudes and interests of the many constituencies that will "get into the act" on issues that involve the company.

Because all the top echelon of senior management officers are potential candidates for the CEO job, they will be expected to fulfill the same requirements. Even their own present jobs will be calling for more of this capability.

So it is not putting square pegs into round holes to give these senior officers a share of the public-affairs involvement. They should have been selected for their jobs with this role in mind.

Incidentally, when we talk about qualifications for public-affairs activity, we are not talking about "charmers" or "smoothies." At one time, these might have been thought of as the stereotypes of the public representative. If anything, those characteristics would be negatives today. Credibility, knowledgeability, and sensitivity all would rank high. Human warmth, yes, but with genuineness and sincerity behind it.

These are not bad qualifications for a senior executive in any context.

XII

Protecting Your Own Physical Plant

In this book on the art of being an executive, I have stressed the *art* element, and I have dwelt at greater length on what an *executive* is. But that leaves a third work, *"being."*

There is little value in knowing about an executive or his art if you are not going to *be*—to survive. Better than that, to flourish and be vital.

I have saved these few words for the end—not as an afterthought or a benediction, but because I would expect them to have more meaning in the light of all that has preceded them. They obviously belong, in terms of priority, ahead of anything else in the book. And I would encourage everyone who reads them to turn quickly, thereafter, back to the front of the book and to flip through the chapter headings again. Picture yourself practicing each facet of this art—as a healthy, vital executive-in-being.

"Job Stress" Depends on Your Values and Priorities

Q Time management and all other disciplines you write about are fine and dandy when you are healthy and in good enough physical condition to keep on top of everything. But how do you survive the stress and pressures of today's business world? They are threats to the health and the very life of an executive. What can he do to protect himself?

A Volumes have been written about stress and how to deal with it. I recommend that you read some of those I'll list at the end of this chapter, because there is always a risk of over-simplifying such a complex subject in the short span of a chapter.

The best that has been written and the best experience of executives who have survived both come down to the same few guiding principles. You can find apparent exceptions to all of them, but you will be safest if you bet on these:

1. It is not stress that kills—but how you respond to it.
   If this were not so, we would not see so many examples

257

of two people exposed to identical pressures where one is thriving on them and the other is falling apart.

2. A corollary is that it is stress *on* the job, not stress *of* the job, that does the damage. There are other factors besides the sheer requirements of the job that put you under pressure and make you feel "stress."

3. A certain amount of stress not only does no harm but is beneficial: your body cannot operate without some stress. What you should avoid, though, is constant, unrelieved tension. The universal rule for healthy functioning is "tense, relax, tense, relax." Your heart does that—so should you. Many of life's ills can be avoided by following that rule.

4. What determines how you react to the stresses of your work is rarely related to the conditions of your work situation. It is much more likely to be found somewhere else in your own life or history.

5. In whatever form they appear, most stress-causing factors involve *anxiety;* and anxiety in turn reflects *fear.* Most often it is fear of failure—but why? Face honestly why you are so fearful, and you have a head start on licking the anxiety.

6. The inner security that shields people against corrosive anxiety has nothing to do with rank or position. Workers at the bottom or middle of the ladder may have more of it than the boss. Security is a function of *values* and *priorities.*

7. A healthy body will often cushion the nerves against bruising pressures. Conversely an unhealthy body can make monumental crises out of the smallest incidents. So put high priority on plenty of sleep, exercise, and sensible intake. If you think the job doesn't leave you time enough for exercise and sleep, you're missing the point: they will increase your efficiency enough that you won't need so much time. I once read that "there are no fat

presidents in the *Fortune* 500." Whether that is literally true or not, it is certain that the physically fit have greater executive-survival power.

Of all these factors, the one that does the most mischief is anxiety, and from the tone of your letter I would suspect that you are a victim of it. Only you can figure out why, but maybe I can give you a few clues that will help you.

What are your priorities—what is most important to you? Is it your own self-esteem, and pride in the excellence of what you do? Or is it how you appear to someone else, what someone else thinks of you—your wife, your neighbors, new members of your club, some girl back home who wouldn't marry you because she didn't think you would ever amount to much? Wanting to "show" someone has probably been more of a motivating factor throughout history than we have ever calculated. And it causes more people to cringe and suffer at the thought of defeat or failure.

You will have more inner security if you will reexamine your values and priorities and make peace with the conflicts between them. More than that, you will be more likely to succeed in your ambitions (and to survive while doing it) if you will be more concerned with professional pride in your performance than with how anyone else rates you. If you can let this be a step on the road to a general sense of self-esteem, self-worth, and self-respect, you won't need to worry about survival.

As to books: Dr. Hans Selye made the world conscious of the concept of stress with his book *The Stress of Life*. A better book for your purpose is his later one *Stress and Distress*, which focuses more on what an individual can do to cope successfully with stress. Even more helpful, because less technical, is *The*

Relaxation Response by Dr. Herbert E. Benson of the Harvard Medical School faculty.

An earlier book by Dr. Edmund Bergler, *How to Reduce Your Tensions,* is heavier going but has an excellent list of "Ten Practical Rules of Reducing Intolerable Tensions to Tolerable Nuisances." This is an adequate goal for most of us.

Epilogue

As the final words in this book, I can go back and expand a bit on the eighth of Lundborg's Laws (see page 90), "Keep Your Motor Tuned and Your Oil Changed."

These words were originally addressed to a conference of all the managers in our bank, but they fit equally well in any company:

"More simply, stay healthy. I suspect there are some of us who take better care of the $6,000 automobile in the garage than we do of ourselves.

"I'm not going to try here to give you any extensive rules of health. In the first place, the rules are well known and you know them as well as I do. In the second place, my son, who is a doctor, would be amazed if he thought I was practicing medicine without a license. But I think he would agree with me that one of the cardinal rules would be the management of time. When you manage it, save time to keep that marvelous machine that is yourself well tuned and maintained.

"There is a charming little story about a Japanese artist who painted a picture on a fairly large canvas. Down in one corner was a tree and on the limbs of the tree were some birds—but all the rest of the canvas was bare. When he was asked if he were not going to paint anything more to fill in the rest of the canvas, he said, 'Oh no—I have to leave room for the birds to fly.' So often we fill our lives so full that there is no room for the birds to fly.

"And our ability to live up to any of the other principles we've talked about today rests finally with our ability to live up to this last one.

"Have outside interests, for a change of pace. You will profit and so will your family. And so in fact will the bank, for you will bring to us a more balanced and broader perspective on your own job. But when you do take on outside activities, be sure you know your capacity—know your limits—and stay within them. Don't take on more than you can do well. Otherwise you'll do everything poorly and drive yourself into an early grave in the process.

"Remember—you can't run your job from a hospital bed, and it is impossible to be a success in the cemetery."

Index

Index